USING NONFICTION IN THE CLASSROOM

Eileen M. Burke and Susan Mandel Glazer

SCHOLASTIC
PROFESSIONAL BOOKS

New York • Toronto • London • Auckland • Sydney

To all those who've cared, and to those who still do
Eileen and Susan

Copyright ©1994 by Eileen M. Burke and Susan Mandel Glazer
Cover by Vincent Ceci
Design by Vincent Ceci
ISBN 0-590-49352-3
Printed in USA
12 11 10 9 8 7 6 5 4 3 2 1

TABLE OF CONTENTS

Our purpose in writing this text is to introduce you, our readers, to using nonfiction in your classroom. We pondered the format and writing style for presenting the manuscript in order to find the tone that would best suit nonfiction materials. We pondered, too, the selection of books used to share the strategies best suited for middle grade students. Hours of conversations and our joint years of experience in education (70 together) resulted in a manuscript that illustrates an integrated approach to promoting inquiry in the classroom through quality nonfiction. The text includes vignettes describing children and teachers using nonfiction. These vignettes illustrate how activities can lead one to another in natural ways. As you read the vignettes throughout the text, and as you engage in nonfiction activities in your own classroom, you will note the range of skills and understandings that can be strengthened by involvement with nonfiction. This text confirms that high quality nonfiction books and instructional strategies used in a healthy, nurturing classroom environment can go a long way toward promoting learning in all areas of the curriculum.

We are grateful to the wonderful children who attend the Center for Reading and Writing at Rider College in New Jersey and extend a special thank you to—Franklin Moore, Theresa Miele, Kristel Slawinski, Mark Jones, JoAnn Wang, Matthew Anderegg, Arne Roomann-Kurrik and their parents Katrin-Kaja Roomann, Kathy Anderegg, Wardell Robinson-Moore, Terry J. Miele, Rhonda Slawinski, Patricia Jones, and Huey-Wen An Wang for permitting us to use illustrations that show, so well, products resulting from effective classroom activities. Our work would not have been possible without the "push and encouragement" provided by our enthusiastic editor, Terry Cooper. Her desire to produce "the best" for teachers for the sake of children is admirable. Last, we thank each other, again, for the many hours of pleasurable professional interactions that only a project like this can spur.

—EMB
—SMG

Five students gather around a classroom table full of books. They pick and browse. Questions and comments flow.

"What does it mean that turtles have lived for nearly two hundred million years?" Ramon asks. He is stunned by the number. "Two hundred million years," he repeats, shaking his head. Ramon is one of your most curious students. He likes facts. They tell him things he wants to know. Facts also tell him things he doesn't even know he wants to know.

"I like these pictures of horses," says Muriah. **"Who is Rosa Bonheur?"** Muriah loves horses. In fact her father tells her that she suffers from a strange disease called "horse-itis." Muriah has just discovered a French artist who loved horses too and who painted powerful pictures of them. Muriah smiles as she looks at one of Rosa Bonheur's most famous paintings called "The Horse Fair" in the book by Robyn Montana Turner.

"What happens to my letter after I put it in the mailbox?" Dominic asks. He has penpals all over the world. His father is in the navy and Dominic has traveled and lived in many countries. He is curious about how, exactly, his letters reach his penpals and how theirs come to him. He would like to follow a letter from writer to reader. When he takes his question to his teacher and his librarian, they help him use the card catalog and the computer. Later, Dominic walks away happily with **Hail the Mail** tucked under his arm.

"They say milk is not good for you but my mother always tells me to drink it. Who's right?" Tamara is confused. She is one of a group of students talking about what is good to eat and what is not. Her question is one of many that result from conflicting information that students hear or read. This time, a newspaper article seems to contradict what Tamara's mother has told her. Now Tamara wants the facts.

"What makes this work?" Marcie stares at the calculator in her hand. Her question is no surprise. Like Dominic, Marcie is curious about a lot of things. Right now, she wants to know why it is that when she presses a number, it flashes at the top of the calculator. She is also wondering how the calculator remembers to add that number to the next one she pushes. Nobody seems to have a ready answer but the librarian points to a book called **The Way Things Work** and sure enough, Marcie finds "calculator" in the index.

You have observed these five students of yours during their "pick and browse" time. You have heard their questions and comments. They are interested; they are curious. No matter what provoked their curiosity; they want answers; they want information; they want facts.

You are delighted. You know from your experience in the classroom that children's natural curiosity is your strongest aid in teaching: it moves children from what they know to what they don't know. You want to keep the curiosity of Ramon, Muriah, Dominic, Tamara, and Marcie alive and well. After all, that's a big part of what learning is all about.

You know, too, that today's children live in a world of rapid change. To survive in it and to understand it, they will need to find and sift through much information. "Is milk good for you or isn't it?" Tamara asks. "Are you sure turtles lived for two hundred million years?" Ramon wants to be certain.

What kinds of materials supply the information that Ramon, Muriah, Dominic, Tamara, Marcie and others are searching for? What kinds of materials keep curiosity alive and well?

Nonfiction materials do—books, magazines, newsletters, newspapers, atlases, almanacs, encyclopedias, illustrations, photographs, documents. These are some of the types of factual materials that satisfy and spur curiosity. It is such materials—their place and use in the classroom—that this book addresses.

CHAPTER ONE

WHY USE NONFICTION IN YOUR CLASSROOM?

In this Information Age, your children need to be informed about a range of topics. At the personal level, they need information about how to maintain good health. Tamara's question is a perfect example. At the social level, they need to know more about how people work together on a task. Dominic's question about mail reflects a search for such information.

Today, students need information that will help them understand the cultures of their own classmates. They are tomorrow's government; they

need to know how best to participate in political processes. They need to know about buying and selling, saving and spending. Certainly they need information about careers and lifestyle options.

The increasing use of machines, from gadgetry to sophisticated technology, stimulates questions like Marcie's about how things work. The need for information is constant. Your children may not always know that they are seeking information, but as they engage in viewing television, listening to the radio, reading general and special-interest magazines, they are actively engaged in a search to know more. Teachers, librarians, and parents can help students in their search. Guiding students toward high-quality nonfiction is worth the time because nonfiction:

- satisfies **and** broadens curiosity;

- provides for depth **and** breadth of information and opens the way for further inquiry;

- offers accurate information and documents such accuracy;

- provides models for concise writing;

- provides visuals that clarify facts;

- demonstrates the need for the logical organization of facts;

- challenges readers to read critically;

- expands vocabulary; and

- offers options to children who prefer fact to fiction.

NONFICTION SATISFIES AND BROADENS CURIOSITY

Nothing spurs learning so intensely and directly as curiosity. You know this so you capitalize on it in your planning and in your teaching.

You have heard students discuss buildings and houses and you've seen their curiosity sparked by the title, **Round Buildings, Square Buildings & Buildings That Wiggle Like a Fish.** Such a title compels children to investigate further. When they do, their attention is held by full-color photographs and, in trying to find out about how buildings **can** wiggle, they digest a great deal of information about buildings all over the world and about architecture in general. Only careful reading—well into the book—will give them the answer to why some buildings wiggle.

As you observe your class exploring other books, you find that those like **Tree, Simple Science Says Take One Balloon,** and **How We Learned the Earth Is Round** supply answers immediately. In **Tree,** children find the answer to the question, "What is a tree?" on the first page. They also find out about the great variety of trees that exist.

In **Simple Science Says Take One Balloon,** Melvin Berger has children remove the balloon attached to the inside back cover and get to work immediately in making a balloon rocket, a balloon submarine, a balloon trumpet, and many other creations that testify to the balloon as a wonderful "tool of science." You are definitely going to involve everyone in these experiments. Students will delight in thinking of the balloon as a science tool, and through Berger's suggestions, they'll prove that it is precisely that.

In **How We Learned the Earth Is Round,** Patricia Lauber sets to work immediately to identify the puzzling questions raised by people over many years as they viewed the earth from prairies, mountains, and seashores and wondered about the evidence before their eyes. Using simple classroom materials, children can demonstrate for themselves what happens to a ship (made from eraser, toothpick, and paper) as it is moved over the curved surface of the earth (a big ball). She involves children in other such simple experiments so they can actually see that the earth is round, how long it took

to prove that fact, and how marvelous it is to have today's NASA photographs that clearly show the curve of the earth.

Children interested in seasons, trees, balloons, a round world, and simple experiments will be fascinated by these books. Their fascination with simple experiments may lead to the notion of testing their own observations. Simple experiments with magnets can follow simple experiments with balloons. **Nonfiction both satisfies and expands curiosity.**

NONFICTION PROVIDES BREADTH AND DEPTH OF INFORMATION

Your own exploration of books has convinced you of the range and depth of information they contain. And you see that when your student Alfie reads **Tree,** he discovers that there are broadleaved trees, coniferous trees, and special kinds of broadleaved trees that grow in the tropics. He also reads about bits of mythology and cultural customs related to trees. This sends him to sources that will tell him about the uses of laurel, holly, and spruces at various times and in various cultures. It may also send him to you and to the librarian for the complete legend of Daphne (and so into Greek mythology) and for information about when trees began to be used at Christmas time (and so into cultural and religious customs). Alfie's search for facts has led him into folklore as well as cultural and religious history. He is finding out more and more and is manufacturing more and more questions that need answers.

Karen, who delightedly participated in all the experiments described in **How We Learned the Earth Is Round,** is now searching for more facts about Columbus and Magellan and their journeys. She also seems intrigued by the old maps she has come upon as she browses in other books.

Nonfiction can extend the range of inquiry by the breadth of content it provides. Questions grow as answers themselves lead to new questions. Through **Tree,** Alfie is making connections he never expected. Karen too has both broadened and deepened her knowledge of Columbus' and Magellan's

journeys and she has acquired an interest in old maps. **Nonfiction provides both breadth and depth of information.**

NONFICTION OFFERS ACCURATE INFORMATION AND DOCUMENTS SUCH ACCURACY

When children ask "Who said so?" and "How do you know?" they are seeking to be sure about what they are reading. Like Ramon, they want confirmation. Nonfiction prompts these kinds of questions. In an Information Age, questions concerning the accuracy of facts are not only appropriate, they are vital. Tamara, for example, raised questions when she was faced with contradictory information.

Children need to be guided to check their sources of information. "Who said so?" and "How do you know?" force teachers and children to check for the credentials of the people who are writing and illustrating the nonfiction they read.

The number and nature of the acknowledgments cited in **The Visual Dictionary of Art** is most impressive. Children see quickly that there were many "authors" with different specialities who helped to compile the Dictionary. Muriah will find a very brief notation about Rosa Bonheur if she remembers that Rosa Bonheur was really named Marie Rosalie Bonheur as Robyn Turner had mentiioned.

In **Himalaya,** the experiences of the author as a writer and photographer who has lived with the Sherpas and Tibetans in Himalaya document the facts she presents. Children find that she is also an experienced author who has written and photographed for **National Geographic** and for **The New York Times.**

Russell Freedman's **Lincoln: A Photobiography** is strongly documented. Evidence of all kinds— old photographs, memoirs, scraps of speeches and prints—about Lincoln and by Lincoln strongly support the information Freedman conveys. The variety of evidence sends a strong message to children that lives can be traced and shared through many different types of doc-

uments. So when children begin to talk about and write about their own lives, they will want to support their statements with all kinds of documents. **Nonfiction offers accurate information and documents such accuracy.**

NONFICTION PROVIDES MODELS FOR CONCISE WRITING

Facts can surprise. Ramon was certainly surprised by the age of the turtle. Writers of nonfiction can depend on the power of facts themselves to appeal to the reader. That's why they state the facts simply and naturally. "Some fish can climb trees," says Seymour Simon in his **Animal Fact/Animal Fable.** Students are astonished and unbelieving. After they declare the statement "fable," they turn the page to find that, in the case of the mud skipper, it is fact.

The organization of **Animal Fact/Animal Fable**—simple statement and illustration on one page followed by facts proving or disproving the statement on the back of the page—is both challenging and logical. Children can use such organization as a model for their own presentations of fact. They might summarize historical information they have been studying into Historical Fact/Historical Fable books and challenge each other to label and then prove or disprove the statements they made.

Writers like Melvin Berger, Joanna Cole, Jim Arnosky, Seymour Simon, Gail Gibbons, and Franklyn Branley know that the power of a fact is in its accuracy and they let the fact speak for itself. When figurative language helps to make the fact clearer, however, they do not hesitate to use it, as does Seymour Simon in his **Storm.** He begins **Storm** by telling his readers that "We live at the bottom of a blanket of air called the atmosphere."

The writer of nonfiction has a special challenge. Facts, though sometimes surprising and intriguing, are impersonal. The author has to write in an appealing way even when the topic seems bland. Authors of the **Eyewitness** series, for example, do not hesitate to bring folklore into their discussion of facts. The child reading about **Amazing Birds** is reminded of "fairy tale swans." Details such as the fact that the flamingo's knees, unlike ours, bend

backwards are provided; in illustration and description the phrase "as vain as a peacock" is explained. **Your students will find that nonfiction provides models for concise and appealing writing.**

NONFICTION CLARIFIES FACTS WITH VISUALS

Without the visuals in **Geography A to Z,** concepts of depth, distance, and location would be difficult to understand. An appreciation of Rosa Bonheur's art would be impossible without the illustrations in Robyn Turner's biography. Muriah found this out when she saw "The Horse Fair." Students need the visuals in **The Bard of Avon** to understand Shakespeare's time and the uniqueness of the Globe Theatre.

In **The Rock-Hound's Book** and **Crystal & Gem,** visuals are essential. Color, shape, and surface features of crystals and "rocks" are clarified by the illustrations. Because these are among the distinguishing features of crystal and minerals, the rock-hounds in your classroom could not differentiate one rock or crystal from another without such illustrations.

There is much in nonfiction that requires illustrative support for clarity and full understanding. High-quality visuals draw readers immediately; their impact is strong. Not only is the presence of visuals in much nonfiction critical, it may also be, for browsing children, what initially draws them to the text. Neither the value nor the quality of visuals in nonfiction should be underestimated. **Nonfiction provides visuals that clarify facts.**

NONFICTION DEMONSTRATES THE NEED FOR LOGICAL ORGANIZATION

Sometimes nonfiction deals with topics so broad or so complex that only the careful labeling and logical organization of such information can make it manageable and clear. Children can appreciate the information only because it is carefully organized.

Books like **Klondike Fever** and **The Age of Chivalry** are rooted in histo-

ry. For such books, a sequential or chronological organization makes sense. So it is that in **Klondike Fever,** your student Jim reads on the first line of the first page that Robert Henderson scooped up a pan of gravel and sand from a remote creek near the Klondike River in Canada in 1896 and found gold at the bottom of the pan. From such an unlikely discovery began a fever that overtook a continent.

In **The Age of Chivalry,** the author treats the two hundred years between 1200 and 1400 A.D., by describing the "power and people" first. Then she goes on to discuss separately "those who fight," "those who work," and "those who pray" in different chapters, concluding with a chapter on knowledge and power. The strong class divisions within the society of the times make this structure sensible. The child reader comes away with solid information about the social makeup of the times.

In some nonfiction, the major topic is presented and a logical break-down of it follows. **Kites Sail High** defines verbs and distinguishes active, less active, linking, auxiliary, and irregular as types of verbs, and then speaks of the moods and voices of verbs.

In **Books** & **Libraries,** Knowlton not only uses historical eras to trace the beginning of libraries and books but also notes the geographical areas in which the development of libraries and books took place.

Some books make the best sense when they begin with major gener-alizations about the topic and conclude with many examples, as in **The Rock-Hound** text and **Crystal & Gem**. How-to books, such as recipe and craft books, must be presented sequentially to be useful.

The alphabet, the calendar, and number sequences are often used to organize information. Whatever the structure decided upon, however, **nonfic-tion demonstrates the need for logical organization.**

NONFICTION CHALLENGES READERS TO READ CRITICALLY

Nonfiction readers read carefully for many reasons. One powerful reason is that they need to use the information they find to make something; to understand a concept, an age, an historical event, a person; to produce a letter, a report, a play; or simply to satisfy their curiosity.

Reading critically means reading carefully; it also means evaluating the information presented. It is important to foster in children the authority to raise questions about the credentials of those who write and illustrate nonfiction. Critical reading also means looking carefully at the way the information is organized, the manner in which it is written, the breadth and depth of it as well as the documentation the author provides.

To be critical readers, children go beyond compiling and interpreting information. They analyze it, synthesize it, and apply it. Some nonfiction challenges the child to exhibit all of these skills; some, a few such skills. Often it is the strategy that teachers use with nonfiction that, focusing on certain skills, helps children to develop and maintain them. Chapters 4 and 5 recommend many strategies for use with nonfiction in the classroom. Skills developed by these strategies are identified at the end of each chapter. **Nonfiction challenges readers to read critically.**

NONFICTION EXPANDS VOCABULARY

As Jackie studies **Castle** she meets words like **corbel, embrasure,** and **merlon.** In **The Hidden Life of the Desert** your students meet the desert iguana, the Gila monster, the diamondback rattlesnake, the saguaro cactus, and the kangaroo rat. In **Marco Polo** readers come upon the Mongols, the Great Buddha, Kublai Khan, and others.

Vocabulary grows through nonfiction. So do concepts. Connecting new words to known words, words to ideas, ideas to other ideas, ideas to past experiences—all of this activity builds a strong network for learning. **Nonfiction expands vocabulary.**

NONFICTION OFFERS AN OPTION TO CHILDREN WHO PREFER FACT TO FICTION

In your classroom you will find some children more entranced by fact than by fable, by reality than by fantasy. A list of classroom favorites is more likely to contain some nonfiction titles if such books have been accessible to children and have been consistently shared with them. Questions throughout **USING NONFICTION IN THE CLASSROOM** attest to the hunger of children for information and the glee and nourishment they derive from facts found and shared.

You may find that some children do not cope with narrative—with its imaginative, figurative phrases and generally longer sentences—as well as they do with more briefly stated facts. They are at home with brevity and expository writing more than they are with the language of story. In addition, the feeling of making facts their own, of controlling information is a powerful sensation. Some children will seek this kind of experience again and again.

All children need to experience excellent models of expository as well as narrative writing. Nonfiction helps to make this possible because **nonfiction offers an option to children who prefer fact to fiction.**

In summary, you will want to use nonfiction in your classroom because it satisfies and stimulates the curiosity of your children; it provides depth and breadth of information that is documented and accurate; it provokes further inquiry and critical reading. It provides models of concise and careful writing, of logical organization and a variety of clarifying illustrative material. It sets examples of clear, high-quality information writing.

The checklist that follows will help you evaluate nonfiction. "Yes" answers identify books that are appropriate and are of high quality. "No" answers raise questions about the quality and appropriateness of the material.

CRITERIA FOR SELECTING NONFICTION MATERIALS

	Yes	No
Satisfies and broadens child's curiosity	❏	❏
Provides depth and/or breadth of information	❏	❏
Offers current information*	❏	❏
Documents the accuracy of information	❏	❏
Provides models of concise writing	❏	❏
Provokes further inquiry	❏	❏
Clarifies text through visuals	❏	❏
Presents information in logical form	❏	❏
Requires critical reading	❏	❏
Expands vocabulary	❏	❏
Appeals to those children who prefer fact to fiction	❏	❏

*Books about topics that do not continuously change over time such as those about seasons, simple machines, landforms, and animal life, do **NOT** require that information be updated daily, monthly, or even yearly. Such books remain "current" for long periods of time.

CHAPTER TWO

HOW WILL YOU KNOW QUALITY NONFICTION MATERIALS WHEN YOU SEE THEM?

Nonfiction materials come in many different formats. Not only are there books and magazines, but newspapers, newsletters, almanacs, atlases, encyclopedias, and documents that present factual

information. You will recognize quality nonfiction materials by many of the characteristics discussed in Chapter 1.

Quality nonfiction materials are full of facts; they are accurate; they are written in concise form; they are organized logically; they provide much illustrative material; and very often they contain specialized vocabulary. In this chapter we offer examples of these characteristics as they are found in a variety of high-quality texts and formats.

FACTS

Nonfiction is full of facts—all kinds of facts—facts about today, facts about yesterday, and even facts about tomorrow. These facts offer an amazing range of information. Not only do they tell Ramon about turtles but they tell Shauna about **A Medieval Feast** and help Donna discover that **Germs Make Me Sick!** The local newspaper annouces the discovery of fossils in the community and Lauber's **Dinosaurs Walked Here and Other Stories Fossils Tell** describes what that may mean.

Facts spring from many sources: for example, some can be found in museum tapestries and old illuminated manuscripts as in **A Medieval Feast.** Some have roots in fossil bones, shells, and tracks of extinct animals as in **Dinosaurs Walked Here and Other Stories Fossils Tell.** Still others can be found in the local gas station as in **Fill It Up!** To support his life of Lincoln, Russell Freedman in **Lincoln: A Photobiography** found facts in photographs and artwork of the time, and in memoirs and scraps of writing.

Facts are what nonfiction is all about. They come from many sources and appear in different formats. You and your students rely on facts. They must be accurate.

ACCURACY

High-quality nonfiction is always accurate. How can you tell that you can rely on the facts provided?

Publishers of nonfiction materials want to assure you that you can

depend upon their publications, so they supply you with information about the author's expertise and experience on the dustjackets of books, in the introductory pages, in the preface, or throughout the materials.

You and your students can believe in the accuracy of the nonfiction materials you are reading when:

- information is given about the author's and illustrator's expertise and experience;

- information is provided about the experts, if any, who were consulted during the writing of the materials;

- major references are cited throughout the text and in the bibliography; and

- materials are current.

Over time, authors, illustrators, and photographers as well as specific series of books may earn a reputation for accuracy. Authors such as Russell Freedman, Melvin Berger, Joanna Cole, Gail Gibbons, Patricia Lauber, Helen Sattler, and Franklyn Branley; photographers such as Jill Krementz, George Ancona, and Jerome Wexler; and illustrators such as Piero Ventura, Leonard Kessler, and David Macaulay have established reputations for accuracy and detail. You and your students will begin to recognize these names.

Series such as the **Let's Read and Find Out Series,** the **First Look at...Series** and the **Eyewitness Books** are among those that have achieved a reputation for careful research and accuracy.

CONCISE FORM

Individual facts are units of accurate information. Their power rests not only in their content but in their clear, generally brief form. It is such concise writing that grips the reader's mind and imagination. Your students need

models of succinct composition in order to develop skill in expository writing. Fiction can help them to write narration; nonfiction can help them write exposition.

Sometimes concise form and imaginative thought merge in the titles and presentations of nonfiction books. Children then find it especially difficult to resist picking up, browsing, and then reading such books. Pithy titles such as **Tree Trunk Traffic, River Ran Wild, Animals Have Cousins Too,** and **The Buck Stops Here** immediately attract students to the content inside.

LOGICAL ORGANIZATION

Facts are much more useful and more easily processed by readers if they are served in an organized fashion.

Sometimes a quick glance at the table of contents, chapter, and section headings show how nonfiction is organized and can help your student gain a sense of the whole topic. In books like **Under the Sea from A to Z** and **Geography from A to Z** the reader discovers from the titles that information is somehow going to be organized according to the letters of the alphabet. In **Under the Sea from A to Z,** the child reads factual descriptions of sea life from anemones to zebrafish. In **Geography from A to Z,** really a pictorial glossary, the reader moves from archipelago to zone.

Another "natural" organizational structure is the months of the year. In **Nature All Year Long,** Clare Walker Leslie starts with January and, through illustrations and descriptions, presents many facts unique to each month. She summarizes information in concise form by providing a brief list of major facts in a colored rectangle at the end of the four-page presentation about each month. Such summaries help your children retain information.

Natural to books about art and craft work is the description of the process from beginning to final product. In **The Pottery Place,** Gail Gibbons describes the process of potterymaking from the time the dry clay is received by the potter to the delivery of the finished pieces to the gift shop for exhibit and sale. The entire process is illustrated and narrated step by step.

In **Sarah Morton's Day,** the text starts with early morning and concludes at evening. This is life in the day of a Pilgrim girl. Carefully detailed and photographed, the organization is dictated by the focus on one day.

In **The President's Cabinet and How It Grew,** Nancy Winslow Parker treats her topic in a strictly chronological fashion as would be predicted from the title. Starting with a humorous and pictorial definition of what the President's Cabinet is not, the author quickly describes the growth of the Cabinet over the years. Children read about the expansion of the Cabinet from George Washington to George Bush.

In many reference books, information is organized by category and children may need help in finding exactly what they seek. Finding an organizational structure for such a compilation of diverse facts as appear in **The Guinness Book of Records** must have been a major challenge. What the authors decided upon were such categories as "The Earth and Space," "The Living World," "The Human Being," "The Human World," and other very broad topics. Such books of facts require detailed indexes or readers would never be able to locate the information they need. To guide children in the use of such books is to help them to develop a lifetime skill in thinking through the possible categories under which facts may be found.

ILLUSTRATIVE MATERIAL

When narration is not enough to clarify nonfiction, drawings, photographs, headings, highlighting, color, even paper engineering (foldouts, tabs, flaps) may be needed.

Certainly it is David Macaulay's drawings that are the heart of such books as **Cathedral** and **Castle.** These drawings entrance students like Jackie and define visually for her "corbel," "embrasure," and other terms.

It is Jerome Wexler's photographs that clarify and support Joanna Cole's careful descriptions of **A Bird's Body.**

Nonfiction materials give you the opportunity to help your students "read"

illustrative materials in order to glean all the information they offer. You know that sometimes it is the strong appeal of remarkable visuals that invite children to sit and stare and think about the book in their hands. You've watched Brian select and become totally absorbed in the outstanding colored photographs in **Chameleons: Dragons of the Trees** while Sean commented on the totally pictorial **The Story of a Castle.**

You have shared **Leonardo Da Vinci** with your class and heard the "ahs" and ohs" when the pages literally popped up with Leonardo's inventions.

SPECIALIZED VOCABULARY

Nonfiction often requires a special vocabulary. To appreciate any topic fully, terms must be understood. Special terms are defined in nonfiction materials in different ways. They may be defined:

> • as they are introduced. In **Books and Libraries**, new terms are printed in italics and defined as soon as they are introduced;
>
> • as part of captions or as additions to labels outside the main narrative. This occurs in **The Magic School Bus** books and in some of the **Eyewitness** books.
>
> • in a special glossary at the back of the book. In **History of Art for Young People**, you have shown your class a glossary of terms at the end of the text and noted with them a list organized by chapters for further reading.

No matter how they are presented, new terms need to be defined and made clear to readers. This sometimes means that they need to be clarified by visual representation.

In summary, when the facts in nonfiction are accurate, when the writing is concise and logically organized, when narrative and illustrations support each other, and when new terms are clearly defined, nonfiction is at its best.

CHAPTER THREE

WHAT ENVIRONMENTS BEST SUPPORT THE USE OF NONFICTION?

An environment that says "Come here. See what I have to offer" invites children into nonfiction. Field trips to museums, to farms, to industrial centers and other sites; experts who discuss their work and hobbies; even the physical arrangement of the classroom can invite children into exploring nonfiction.

FIELD TRIPS

Your friend, Ms. Elsey, often takes her fourth graders on field trips. The latest one was to the American Museum of Natural History. The trip was planned for several reasons. Children were interested in New York City, and they had been reading about the great museums in cities in the United States.

Ms. Elsey was interested in heightening children's interest in several content areas. She had begun to use more and more nonfiction books and field trips to develop concepts in content area studies. The museum, she felt, would spur interest in social studies and the sciences.

As the school bus pulled up to the museum, all eyes focused on the great stairway to the front door. Children trotted off the bus and once inside the museum, Ms. Elsey knew that she had chosen the right field trip. All eyes were wide, almost awed, and attentive. One look at Franklin's face, for instance, was enough for Ms. Elsey to realize how surprised he was. Ms. Elsey was delighted. Something finally sparked Franklin's interest.

Franklin and his classmates were fascinated by the Brown Bear exhibit, and the one featuring how our bodies work, but the highlight of the day was certainly the dinosaur exhibit.

Every student in Ms. Elsey's class kept a journal. This was a vehicle for sharing ideas and feelings candidly with their teacher. The morning after the trip to the museum, Franklin wrote a letter to Ms. Elsey about his experiences at the museum.

Franklin's Handwritten Letter to Ms. Elsey

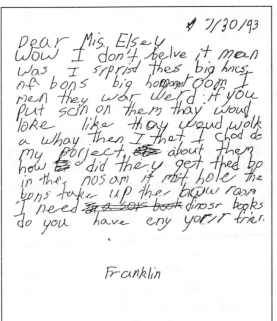

(Translation of Franklin's Letter)

Dear Ms. Elsey,

Wow! I don't believe it. Man, was I surprised! These hunks of bones, big, humongous room, I mean they were weird. If you put skin on them, they would look like they would walk away. Then I thought I could do my project about them. How did they get the bones in the museum? It must [be a big] hole. The bones take up the whole room. I need dinosaur books. Do you have any?

Your friend,

Franklin

What an opportunity! Ms. Elsey's observations of Franklin during the museum excursion and Franklin's letter confirmed his interest. Franklin's request for a book was her cue to search for some wonderful nonfiction books. Putting many books about dinosaurs in the classroom library was one way to entice Franklin into nonfiction.

Franklin's request for books was a major step forward because Franklin disliked reading. He especially shied away from his social studies and science textbooks. Ms. Elsey was delighted in his interest in dinosaurs. His interest was strong; she was sure he would read to find answers to those questions he wrote in his letter to her. Nonfiction would provide the answers and would also further develop some reading, writing, and study skills, especially those necessary for writing research reports—a curriculum goal.

ARRANGEMENT OF CLASSROOM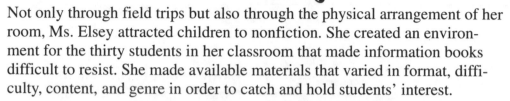

Not only through field trips but also through the physical arrangement of her room, Ms. Elsey attracted children to nonfiction. She created an environment for the thirty students in her classroom that made information books difficult to resist. She made available materials that varied in format, difficulty, content, and genre in order to catch and hold students' interest.

In her attempt to maximize the learning from nonfiction, Ms. Elsey encouraged her students to work in pairs and in small groups. She arranged furniture, equipment, and materials so that different groups of children would have adequate space for collaborative work. She also realized that the physical arrangement of furniture and materials had to respect both children who could sit for long periods of time and those who needed to "wiggle" when they read.

She reviewed the centers she already had in her classroom—classroom library, media center, conference center, and display centers—asking herself how she might highlight nonfiction in each. All centers were used for reading, writing, and research efforts, and for display and storage. She realized early on that she would need to support work in nonfiction with a new center which she would call the Reference Center.

CLASSROOM LIBRARY

This center is the focal place for Ms. Elsey's informational materials. Her collection contained fiction and nonfiction but, for social studies and science projects, focused particularly on nonfiction. In reviewing her collection of books and materials, Ms. Elsey wanted to be sure that the nonfiction would both answer students' questions and stir further searching and questioning. Her shelves contained a variety of formats, narrative and pictorial. There were heavily illustrated books as well as three-dimensional (pop-up and pull-out) types; there were a few copies of newspapers as well as a special interest magazine. There were picture books, historical texts, historical fiction, biographies, autobiographies, and many reference materials.

In selecting materials, Ms. Elsey used the checklist on page 19, "Criteria for Selecting Nonfiction Materials."

Ms. Elsey believes she should have at least five nonfiction books for each child in her classroom. She counts the number of nonfiction books and reviews the collection to make sure it includes books that focus on many content areas—social studies, science, math, art, music, and drama. She consults with the school librarian so that the classroom and the school collections complement each other.

There are few specialized magazines such as those that focus on sports, or entertainment, or on student concerns such as attracting friends, doing well in school, or dealing with siblings. Ms. Elsey plans to look into the availability of, and quality of, such materials and expects to order such journals to round out her collection.

Collections of materials on particular topics and authors are best exhibited in the classroom library center. The works of Jean Craighead George are admired by Ms. Elsey's students so she will feature this author in her next display. She also considers how to change displays frequently to spark student interest.

As she considers her library materials, Ms. Elsey realizes she has given little attention to the special and personal interests of students as they express them in their personal reading periods or in their journals. Informal conversations with children in the classroom, in the lunchroom, on the playground, in the auditorium, in the library, and other school locations also indicate interests.

During informal times, Ms. Elsey always talks about her own interests beyond the curriculum in order to serve as a model for children to share theirs. When they do share, she quickly jots down these interests in her daily plan book. She tries to find topics that several children might be interested in in order to encourage peer and collaborative inquiry.

MEDIA CENTER

Computers and printers, cassette recorders with earphones, and radios have been collected and are available here. This equipment makes it possible for Ms. Elsey's students:

- to listen and note information from tapes of books on topics being studied;

- to listen and compile information from talks by experts on topics relevant to the curriculum and to their interests;

- to respond in discussions and in writing to information they've heard; and

- to become aware of additional nonfiction materials to confirm information they've heard.

Ms. Elsey will review materials and equipment here for content range, curriculum appropriateness, and student interests.

CONFERENCE CENTER

This is a small space that provides privacy for two to four children to gather and share ideas. Conferences may be among students or between teacher and students. The conference is a collaborative interaction during which those who meet share and learn from each other.

All of the children in the class had been studying the plight of the slaves in the 1800's in America. Each day, Ms. Elsey read sections of the book **Letters From a Slave Girl,** by Mary Lyons. She particularly likes the work of Mary Lyons, who is an author of both fiction and nonfiction. All of Ms. Lyons' books are based on historical events.

One morning two nine-year-old girls sit in the Conference Center discussing the book. Ms. Elsey overheard the following conversation which seemed to demonstrate to her how interaction supports and enlivens the use of nonfiction materials for content learning.

Jennifer: I took this book because Ms. Elsey read it to us. Ya know, all it is is a bunch of letters. I really like it. Anyway (shrugging her shoulders) I learned a lot about the slaves. Gosh, it was awful to be a slave. Harriet, one of the girls who was a slave —she wrote the letter.

Samantha: What do you mean a bunch of letters?

Jennifer: That's what it is. Don't you remember, when Ms. Elsey read— they were letters. See. She opens the book and points to a letter. But I learned a lot. Listen. (She reads aloud.)

Samantha: Gosh, you sound real Southern. Let me see that (as she takes the book from Jennifer's hands). I just read a book that is a bunch of letters, too. The name of it was **Letters from Rifka,** and it was a whole bunch of letters from a Russian girl and I learned about the Holocaust a little, from the book.

Jennifer: Oh, I know. **The Diary of a Young Girl** about Anne Frank is like that, and that was the first, and I read it ages ago.

Samantha: Anyway, I think that I am going to write a book; it will be a bunch of letters. And I will tell about all the things I did when I visited my grandmother in New York. I'll write letters to my friend who lives in Montana, so the letters will be real ones, and I will tell her all about my trip and all the things that are in New York. They call it the Big Apple, ya know.

Jennifer: You could make that your social studies project.

Samantha: What do you mean?

Jennifer: Well, Ms. Elsey said we could pick a city and read about it. We need to find out who lives there, ya know, the population...

Samantha: What's that?

Jennifer: You mean the "population"?

Samantha: Yes.

Jennifer: Well those are the people who live there—all different kinds. Ah, I'm not sure how to say it, but there's lots of books in the library about the

population. Anyway, that's a good project and it would be easy to write letters instead of a real research paper.

As she listened to Jennifer and Samantha, Ms. Elsey noted that they certainly were curious and that they:

- talked about using letter format for their own writing;

- inquired further about their topics and formats for presentation;

- seemed to understand that their historical presentations needed to be chronological in organization;

- showed interest in words specific to their topics;

- were quick to mention other books written in letter form; and

- were aware they would need to seek other sources for information.

Many times in the past, Ms. Elsey had noted how ideal the Conference Center was for peer tutoring. She saw again today how ideal it was for sharing information and for collaborative work. She was not surprised at the dialogue between Samantha and Jennifer. She had often predicted and confirmed that her students would guide one another in selecting and sharing nonfiction, and in understanding special terms, and that they would share responses to nonfiction. She had observed them helping each other edit written responses to nonfiction and serving as the audience for readers' theater productions and other products based on their work together. The Conference Center proved its worth many times over.

DISPLAY CENTERS

Displaying process and products—drawings, drafts of projects, final editions, notes to classmates, and more—is important for developing communication skills and for sharing information texts. Classroom and corridor bulletin boards and walls, display tables, and classroom corners can be the backdrops for research-in-progress.

Richard responded to the label "SHOW YOU CARE; SHARE." and displayed a diorama he'd constructed, which identified parts of the human body. Other children who produced products followed Richard's lead and added theirs to the Display Center. This continued throughout the school year.

In addition to centers in which work is displayed, children need a place where the tools of writing are kept. This is where they can get pencils, pens, felt-tipped markers, and the paper they need— all sorts of paper—for responding in writing to the nonfiction they read. These tools must be easily accessible. Ms. Elsey created just such a central place. She also stored here materials such as the erasers, toothpicks, paper, and balls that were needed for children to participate in the experiments in **How We Learned the Earth Is Round.**

REFERENCE CENTER

Samantha and Jennifer needed information about the population of New York City. Annie wanted to know more about the life of Rosa Bonheur. Franklin wanted to know much more about dinosaurs. Ms. Elsey was aware that nonfiction breeds more nonfiction. Reference materials needed to be handy as more and more questions popped up.

Mr. Rob, a colleague who taught a sixth-grade class, had a Reference Center in his classroom. When Ms. Elsey conferred with him, he gave her the following list of materials that were included in his center:

- different dictionaries at different reading levels;

- several thesauruses;

- different versions of world maps with varied projections;

- varied local, city, state and country maps;

- maps with specific political and physical features;

- an atlas;

- at least one almanac;

- pamphlets that identified sources of free resource materials;

- encyclopedias;

- lists of places to visit; and

- lists of the names and addresses of local and state experts in various fields.

As Ms. Elsey looked at the list, she showed surprise at the inclusion of varied local maps. Mr. Rob grinned and shared the following:

"One afternoon, I watched Simon, a twelve-year-old, looking at two maps of this town. I wasn't sure where he got the older of the two maps and I was curious about what he was doing.

"When I asked him, Simon said, 'My grandpop grew up in this town,

but the name of the street he lived on is not on this map. When I told my grandpop about this, he found this old map and gave it to me. I'm trying to find his street on this one. He says it's here.'"

Ms. Elsey pulled together her reference materials. Using Mr. Rob's collection as a guide and Simon's need for old local maps, she realized that she could secure materials from yard sales and from her own attic, as well as order them from available school funds. She might even involve her students in their own attic searches and then help them judge the quality of what they found.

Before collecting materials, Ms. Elsey scheduled a time when she and Mr. Smithson, the school librarian, could discuss fully the school's reference holdings. She and Mr. Smithson spent some time discussing references needed to support the curriculum and themed units and they also considered the interests of fourth through eighth graders.

Mr. Smithson was impressed with the survey Ms. Elsey had taken of her students' interests and wondered if she wouldn't share the form and the results with other teachers—perhaps at a faculty meeting. He would be very interested in the results of a school-wide survey, he said. It would help him in deciding the kinds of materials—fiction and nonfiction—he should order.

As Ms. Elsey spoke with Mr. Smithson, she realized the need for more dialogue with the school librarian. For one thing she learned that, in addition to the school library holdings, she could borrow materials from the county and state library collections. She learned too that a request to borrow materials could be processed much more quickly than she had thought. She began to see the classroom library as a small center of many larger centers available to her.

As he listened to Ms. Elsey relate that she had set up a new Reference Center in her classroom, Mr. Smithson said he would be pleased to work with Mr. Rob and herself as well as other teachers in reviewing the reference materials in their classrooms. Perhaps a checklist might be helpful, he thought, and after some time he worked out the following checksheet for teachers who wished to assess their reference collections.

In summary, nonfiction books are important for recreational as well as for informational reading. Field trips and presentations by experts as well as the physical arrangement of furniture and materials in their classroom enable children and their teacher to enjoy and respond to nonfiction. It is important, when sharing nonfiction with children, that there are sufficient resources—permanent and rotating—to support the questions nonfiction generates. To assure high-quality nonfiction materials and to assess reference collections in classrooms, it is helpful to use checklists.

CHECKLIST FOR EVALUATING CLASSROOM REFERENCE MATERIALS

	Yes	Need More/Comment
Nonfiction materials in my classroom along with those in the school library adequately support the curriculum.	❑	❑
I have several types of the same reference materials: i.e., maps, almanacs, etc., in my classroom.	❑	❑
I used specific criteria when choosing nonfiction materials.	❑	❑
I have in my classroom at least:		
• an encyclopedia	❑	❑
• an almanac	❑	❑
• an atlas	❑	❑
• six dictionaries	❑	❑
• six thesauruses	❑	❑
• content-based magazines, i.e., Sports Illustrated, Ranger Rick, Stone Soup, others	❑	❑
• daily newspapers	❑	❑
• museum publications	❑	❑
As information becomes outdated, I replace it with current materials.	❑	❑
I post names and addresses of sources where needed and timely information.	❑	❑
If a topic is controversial, I select materials that offer different points of view.	❑	❑
I include materials brought in by my students in the Reference Center.	❑	❑
I survey my class to determine students' interests.	❑	❑
The classroom resources and reference collections include student products created in conjunction with content area studies (i.e., narratives, dramatic and slide presentations, artistic endeavors, etc.)	❑	❑

CHAPTER FOUR

WHY READ NONFICTION TO YOUR CLASS?

In previous chapters, we have discussed why using nonfiction in your classroom is enriching, how you can recognize high-quality nonfiction materials when you see them, and what environments best support the use of nonfiction. Now we are ready to consider the best strategies for using nonfiction in the classroom. What kinds of structured activities are most likely to initiate and maintain interest in nonfiction in your students?

In this chapter, we will present and support the use of nonfiction read-aloud sessions. Such sessions, in which a teacher takes time to read aloud an information book to the class:

- support curriculum themes;
- expand student interest in content areas;
- take advantage of a child's spontaneous questions;
- stimulate a need to document facts;
- create interest in areas totally new to the child;
- capitalize on current and local events;
- support report writing; and
- provide practice in finding and researching facts for project completion or story creation.

We believe that reading nonfiction **to** your students is the major strategy for building interest in nonfiction **in** your students. Not only does this stimulate interest in nonfiction and in many content areàs, it results in a great variety of responses from students and helps them to develop many reading and study skills.

The read-alouds which follow offer many examples of how sharing nonfiction aloud with a class enriches curriculum themes, broadens student interest in content areas, supports research skills and report writing, and keeps the school program current.

Because the use of nonfiction is so productive in nurturing the development of many skills, we have noted the specific skills developed through the strategies discussed in Chapters 4 and 5 at the end of each chapter.

For years teachers have read stories, poems, and chants to children but have seldom read nonfiction to them. Is the content of nonfiction books inappropriate for reading aloud? Are topics unappealing? Have we ourselves not searched for nonfiction books to support our own special interests?

We know how contagious enthusiasm is. Each day you and your colleagues rediscover how easily your own eagerness and joy in classroom experiences and content affect your children. Surely your own enthusiasm

for nonfiction can be transmitted to your students. In nonfiction, great ranges of interesting topics abound from eels to electronics, from Picasso to paper-making. Why can't nonfiction read-aloud sessions generate the same kinds of excitement that sharing stories has accomplished in the past?

It can! You can "sell" nonfiction through read-aloud sessions. This chapter tells you why and offers some suggestions.

GETTING READY FOR READ-ALOUDS

You can start by setting aside a regular time for "Nonfiction Read-Alouds." Generally, the books you select coordinate with the content in your social studies, science, mathematics, art, and music programs. They may also sup port student and teacher interests.

You will want to select some books that are short enough to share in a few days; others that will require a longer period of time. You may also want to share a series of nonfiction books written by a single author thus providing continuity in writing style. The consistent style entices reluctant readers to read more because they become comfortable with the author's style and format.

Including fiction as well as nonfiction in preparing for read-alouds can deepen children's interest in content. It can also serve as a springboard for imagining what an animal's life is really like.

READ-ALOUD 1: THE LAST DINOSAUR

Following the visit to the museum Franklin found a copy of Jim Murphy's **The Last Dinosaur** and asked Ms. Elsey to share it with the class.

Ms. Elsey realized the book was ideal in that it enriched a curriculum theme, provided a model for hypothesizing and supporting a hypothesis, and capitalized on student interest. In **The Last Dinosaur,** author Jim Murphy suggests that Triceratops was the last dinosaur.

Students' Responses

Following this sharing, many questions and speculations were voiced about dinosaurs and their last days.

"What made Jim Murphy think the last dinosaur was a Triceratops?" Ms. Elsey asks. After the class hypothesizes, you share the author's "TriceraFacts" section. You listen as students argue Mr. Murphy's position. Many of them agree that the Triceratops was the "best candidate" for the last dinosaur but there were a few who wondered if Triceratops was not outwitted by groups of other types of dinosaurs.

The hunt was on for more books about dinosaurs. Didi found Sattler's **Tyrannosaurus Rex and Its Kin** (1989) and organized the information from the text on a Book Summary card similar to the one following.

Book Summary Card

Title
Author
Publisher
Year of Publication
Important Facts

Other summary cards were soon added for the following books:

Simon, S. **New Questions and Answers About Dinosaurs**

Schlein, M. **Discovering Dinosaur Babies**

Lauber, P. **Living with Dinosaurs**

And the hunt continued.

Abe was delighted to find **What Happened to the Dinosaurs?** Would Branley agree with Jim Murphy? He was excited by that question; he intended to find the answer.

The class was well on its way to a fair compilation of "DinoFacts" as Lynne, one of the students, quickly labeled the box holding the summary cards.

Later, as Ms. Elsey reviewed the sharing of **The Last Dinosaur,** she was amazed at the hypotheses that flowed, the searches for more information that were stimulated, the records that were produced of facts found, and the exciting sharing sessions that were generated. All in all, the read-aloud session was a rich use of class time.

READ-ALOUD 2: THE 13 MOON SERIES

Throughout the year, as part of a continuous study of the environment and ecology, animal fact and animal fiction were visible in many displays. Students were captivated by Jean Craighead George's work, **On My Side of the Mountain,** so when Ms. Elsey heard from the librarian about the **13 Moon Series,** she decided that that would be a perfect set of texts to use for the thematic study of animals. These texts are chock full of facts integrally woven into a fictional story line that enlivens the texts. Fictional narrative seems to accent the facts, intensifying the ability to recall them.

This series is named for the thirteen full (or new) moons that appear yearly. Award-winning author Ms. George has named the thirteen books after thirteen North American animals. Each book focuses on an animal's behavior during a specific month of the year.

Ms. Elsey decides that sharing this series is a wonderful activity for the first several days of each calendar month. Her class quickly begins to look forward to what they call "the animal of the month books." Jean George takes the class, through her books, to Connecticut in September to follow the plight of the male buck; to the Great Plains to follow the eastern mole who roams through extensive networks of tunnels searching for food; to Ohio in December to experience the pursuit of food and warmth by the song sparrow.

Students' Responses

Ms. Elsey's class shows much surprise when they meet the wild pig in Arizona's Sonoran Desert. "A pig in a desert?" asks Lennie. The lost piglet's struggle to avoid many hidden dangers as well as to survive in the dry climate holds the attention of the class. Ms. Elsey remarks later that she saw the same rapt attention to the piglet's plight as she experienced many times in reading fiction to her class.

The **13 Moon** read-aloud excited much interest and sent many of Ms. Elsey's students to reference materials. Richard wanted to know more about the piglet and the mole. His question was echoed by others. In the face of many questions, Ms. Elsey asked Mr. Smithson, the librarian, for help. Mr. Smithson met with the students and showed them the sections in the library that housed nonfiction books and major references. He also pointed to the encyclopedias, **The Larousse Encyclopedia of Animal Life** as well as several titles in the **Eyewitness** Series as being helpful to them in gathering facts about animals.

Before Mr. Smithson left the class to their searching and browsing, he mentioned that there were many books of fiction that contained a wealth of information about specific animals such as **The Yearling, Old Yeller,** and **Where the Red Fern Grows.** There were grins at the mention of **The Yearling:** several students had seen the film. As Mr. Smithson walked away, he knew he would receive requests for these books too and, sure enough, Danny turned back to him and asked to borrow **The Yearling.** "My brother really liked that book. I think I would too."

As Ms. Elsey's students began to gather information about animals, she reminded them that there were facts they already knew from Jean George's books and other prior reading they had done. "Think about what you know about moles, or bucks, or ____ and record that on a book summary card. Then go on to list the new important facts you are finding. Be sure, though, that you check on the accuracy of what you already know."

Ms. Elsey wrote the following suggestion on the chalkboard after talking to several of the children about her idea. Her note to the children was as follows:

Boys and Girls,

After you read your nonfiction book, ask yourself the following questions:

What did I learn?

What do I still want to learn?

Ten-year-old Theresa, who loved reading about animals, had just completed Jean Craighead George's **The Moon of the Mole.** She had obviously read the questions and rephrased them responding to Ms. Elsey's suggestion. Figure 4-1 was written by Theresa immediately after she completed the book. She wrote it in her nonfiction reading log, a notebook. She explained, " I like writing in a log, cause it looks like a book." Theresa and the other children in the class each had a log for recording important information from nonfiction books immediately after they read one. This writing helped the children clarify facts and remember them. This important tool also helped children understand the relationship between reading and writing. Theresa loved reading about animals since her life was enmeshed with them. She had two pets of her own. Each of her siblings had a pet and both parents were veterinarians.

Theresa's Response to Reading

(Translation of Theresa's Response to Reading)

I learned about that moles eat one ounce and a half. Their days are eight hours [long], three hours awake five hours asleep. Their claws turn out for digging. They used to have eyes and ears but they don't need them [because they aren't useful in the ground]. Their enemies are coyote and badger. Their tunnels are only inches; their nose is very useful. Their tail and bottom of their feet have tiny hairs for hearing.

The **13 Moon Series** read-aloud stirred strong motivation and excitement about finding out more about the animals discussed

> Book: The 13 moons The Moon of the Moles
> Author: Jean CRAIGHEAD George
>
> What I Learned From The Book.
>
> I learned about that moles eat 1 oz and half They eat There days are 8 hours 3 hours awake 5 hours asleep There claws turn out for diggin they usto have eyes and ears but they don't need them there enimes are cyotoe and badger There tunnels are only inches There nose is very useful. The tail and the bottom of there feet have tiny hairs for hearing.
>
> What Would You Still Like to Learn more about the moles enimies)
>
> Theresa 10 years old

in the series. In the process of searching for more facts, students arrived at a better understanding of the school library collection, realized that fiction can contribute to the store of facts they've learned, and discovered that it saves time to list what you already know about a topic.

READ-ALOUD 3: THE BUCK STOPS HERE

Mr. Rob reads nonfiction to his students too. One of the titles he wants his students to know about is **The Buck Stops Here** by Alice Provensen. This is the year children are expected to learn about American history, specifically the presidents. In Provensen's book, historical facts are presented in language that invites children into the book's contents. The author serves history

through rhyme and delightful, informative drawings. The rhymes and drawings help students remember the information as they make connections between presidents and the events surrounding their administrations. Poetry, visuals, and facts combine to invite students to compare and contrast administrations.

In **The Buck Stops Here,** each administration is introduced with a couplet. The one about Thomas Jefferson's administration reads: Thomas Jefferson, number Three, Rigged the Sale of the Century.

In the background, there is a drawing of Jefferson with several interwoven illustrations depicting events that occurred while Jefferson was President. These events are labeled and presented in chronological order at the bottom of the page. The catchy rhyme and the detailed drawings force children and adults to listen to, and to look again and again, at each page.

Because of the need for students to see the page, Mr. Rob shares the book with Jim and Richard in the Conference Center first.

Students' Responses

After listening to Mr. Rob and looking at the pages as he read the text aloud, the boys soon took over and began reading aloud to each other pointing to various rhymes and illustrations they wanted to return to. They were so enthusiastic about the text; they wanted to share with everyone. "We'll recite the rhyme," they told Mr. Rob "and everyone will act out an event of each administration. It'll be great," they assured him.

They asked for an overhead projector to share the illustrations with the class and began to invite their classmates to look at the book and choose an administration and an event they would like to act out. Before Mr. Rob knew it, a full-blown historical dramatization was quickly forming in the imaginations of Richard and Jim. They were off and running!

Mr. Rob was startled and pleased at the quick transformation from text to drama. Inevitably, the planning would lead to many more questions, more research, more sharing, more information. He realized that the play

could be a comprehensive synthesis of the study of American history from the Revolution to modern times. It was, in fact, an excellent review of much of the year's social studies program.

Mr. Rob had liked the book; it seemed to meet the criteria he was using to select nonfiction. He was, however, overwhelmed by the enthusiasm with which the book was greeted and the kinds of planning it stimulated. "That was a great idea about reading this book aloud to Jim and Richard first," he congratulated himself. "They just took off from there and the whole class will know its contents well. They'll all use it to plan their 'acts.'"

He looked at George and Don as they probed the text and he heard them remark that there were many other people in the pictures in addition to the presidents. "Who was this Chief Joseph?" George wanted to know. "Who were Rebecca Felton and Jeannette Rankin?" Don asked. The two of them started on an information hunt in the direction of the encyclopedias. Noting their interest, Mr. Rob suggested that they might want to record their findings on "Famous People" cards. Both boys were familiar with baseball cards and liked the "Famous People" card idea. Mr. Rob had cut cardboard into rectangles 3" by 3 1/2". He typed "Famous People Card" at the top of each card and placed them in a box. He pulled one out and began to write a card about Bill Clinton. The boys' excitement was illustrated by the cards that they created shown in Figure 4-2.

Famous People Cards

Herbert Hoover

Bank closings

forecloshers

12 millon un-
'employed

Hoover

franklin Pierce

First Flag flown

trety with Japan

Pierce

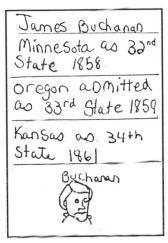

James Buchanan
Minnesota as 32nd
State 1858.

Oregon aDmitted
as 33rd State 1859

Kansas as 34th
State 1861

Buchanan

4-2

READ-ALOUD 4: THE HOUSE I LIVE IN

In Ms. Fernandez' classroom, a month-long interest in buildings had begun when several children in their browsing time had become absorbed in David Macaulay's **Castle, Cathedral,** and **Pyramid.** There had been much discussion about the time, the purpose, the planning, the price of different buildings. At the moment, Melissa is poring over Isadore Seltzer's **The House I Live In.** Seltzer writes about and illustrates many types of houses in our land. He begins with the adobe homes of early American settlers and moves to the contemporary high-rise apartments of our large cities. The houseboat, mobile home, and log cabin are among the homes described through lively illustrations and descriptive text. Melissa wants Ms. Fernandez to share the book with the class.

Ms. Fernandez decides to read it aloud and makes certain everyone sees the illustrations that accompany the descriptions of each house.

Students' Responses

A number of children become very interested in the changing house designs and the historical period in which each house was prominent. Rebecca and Paul think it would be a great idea to make a historical time line of houses so you could see the change over time at a glance. Ms. Fernandez knows the school library also has a copy of the book; she promptly borrows it so that the planners can have two copies for their research. As the time line takes shape, the students decide to write a blurb under each house. The blurbs are summaries of the information from the text and include the students' perceptions about living in each house.

Another group of students are intrigued with the variety of homes represented in the book.

Michael: I never see houses like those around here. All our houses in this town are the same.

Susan: No they're not. Richie's house has no upstairs but mine does.

Allan: I live in a half-house.

Michael: Come on! A half house?

Allan: That's right. My father and mother own one half of the house and our neighbors own the other.

Susan: I never heard of that but then my aunt says she lives in a house and a half 'cause my grandmother has a little apartment attached to my aunt and uncle's house.

Michael: Good grief! A half house and a house and a half. What next?

Michelle: Well, (impatiently) think about it, Michael. Somewhere in the book it said that people build houses that are right for them. (She thumbs through a copy of the book, and reads sections that explain that what was "right" seemed to depend on climate, location, and available materials.)

Annie and Karen are carrying on a conversation of their own while they examine the second copy of the text.

Annie: See this house? (pointing to the picture in the book) It's on stilts because it's on the beach. So the house is up on the stilts. In case the waves are high, the house will stay dry.

Karen: I saw a house on stilts in Long Beach Island. This one (pointing to another picture) looks like it has four legs, but I think there's another one that you can't see from this angle of the picture. The house I saw at the beach had twelve stilts.

Annie: It must have been huge.

Karen: Well, it looked like a hotel. But my Mom told me it was a house because she knows the people who live in it. (Pauses and thumbs through the book.) I like this pink one. When I was in California, my aunt took me to a Spanish restaurant that looked like it. See (holding the book so Annie can see it), the book says that this house was copied from old Spanish churches. They called them missions.

Annie: Let me see that. Oh, I was in San Antonio—that's in Texas—and they had a mission there. That's right! The missions had roofs like the pink one. I wonder why they had those curved doorways.

Both girls continue to examine the book together, chatting as they do.

Annie: What is a "mortar"? Is it the same as a "stonemason"?

Karen: I don't know what "terrace" is.

Annie: Maybe we better write the words in the back of our reading logs.

Karen: Yeah, I guess so. Ms. Fernandez told us to do that if we didn't know a word.

Annie: My Mom says I should always look the words up in a dictionary when I don't know what they mean.

Karen: Ms. Fernandez said to do that too. I'll get one.

Both girls went to the Reference Center and each took a dictionary. They attempted to look up the word "mortar" first. Karen was able to find the word, but Annie could not. Karen copied the first meaning of the word as

it appeared in the dictionary on the page of her notebook where she had written the word. Ms. Fernandez reviewed this page in students' notebooks daily. Students would read the words, and discuss and refer to them within the context of the book in which they appeared. Ms. Fernandez never really knew how to check for students' use of these words. She felt that it was important for children to make the words their own by using them in their oral and written language. She told the children that she would listen to them talk. When they used one of their new words in their conversations at least three times, the word belonged to them. She also used the same "rule of thumb" for writing. When a word was used at least three times in one of their pieces of writing, that word belonged to them. Ms. Fernandez knew that in order to learn new words, children had to use them in functional ways. Vocabulary instruction grew from content area study. Children had to learn new words in order to learn new content.

The informal discussions triggered by read-aloud sessions lead to more inquiry and to vocabulary expansion. Planned discussions or "book talks" are also important for getting the most from the content of nonfiction books. Such talks may take a variety of forms.

Book talk flows naturally from a read-aloud. If the content fascinates, the questions will roll and the planning of extension activities will be imaginative and exciting.

READ-ALOUD 5: MOJAVE

Mr. Rob expected much talk would flow after his sharing of **Mojave,** a book that he felt certain would enable children to view landforms in a totally new, highly imaginative, yet accurate fashion. He was right. Nonfiction can lead to comments, questions, and creative expression. **Mojave** led to all three.

Students' Responses

At first, the class was puzzled by **Mojave.** They had never heard a desert "talk" before. In **Mojave,** the desert itself speaks and feels and thinks. The ecology of the desert is described in the first person, much of the language is

musical and the paintings are arresting. After initial puzzlement, every sixth grader was caught by the words and the paintings.

After a discussion about the book that ranged from awe over the illustrations and interest (even delight on the part of some students) in the idea of having the desert itself talk, "What if _____ could talk?" queries streamed forth. The book talk became highly imaginative. Everyone joined in and Mr. Rob listened. Discussion went on and on.

Rosalie: What if animals could talk?

Danny: In Dr. Doolittle they did.

Karen: It happens at midnight every year on Christmas Eve. That's when all the animals are supposed to be able to talk. But I think it's just a made-up story.
After some talk and laughter about what their own pets might say to them if they could speak, Mr. Rob referred to **Mojave** again and asked,
"What kinds of landforms have we read and talked about this year?"
Students responded with words like "mountains," and "grasslands."

Mr. Rob: Could these be imagined as speakers?

Sandy: Maybe. I think I can think of some things a mountain could say about itself.

Roberta and Shauna joined in and a "mountain" group was formed to do some collaborative writing and editing.

Karen: Robbie, you're a good artist. Would you draw some pictures of mountains to go with what we write?

Questions began to roll about mountain surfaces, inhabitants, age, etc. All in all, Mr. Rob thought the aftermath of reading **Mojave** aloud to his class was unexpectedly productive.

He found that he had to remind the groups that the facts in **Mojave** were not changed because they were written in the first person and in rather poetic language. "Let's be sure we locate accurate facts and after that decide on the best way to share them—first, second, or third person."

READ-ALOUD 6: A RIVER RAN WILD

Sometimes a read-aloud excites questions about local conditions and generates research about the here and now. Ms. Elsey wanted to stimulate just such questions. She left **A River Ran Wild** in the center of a display table and noticed that her children were absorbed with the bookjacket; they were intrigued by the small inserts that frame a scene of natural beauty.

They raised questions about the title, read the flyleaf and the endpaper, and asked her to read it to them.

Students' Responses

After the reading, May asked, with wonder in her voice, "You mean you can **un-pollute** something?"

Following careful picture sharing and discussion, Ms. Elsey's students had many questions:

Can you really clean up dirty rivers and streams?

Can we really clean up the air?

What about cleaning up downtown? It's a mess.

Ms. Elsey: Where can we find information about how to clean up our community?

Brad: Well, the book says it is an "environmental history." Maybe we can look up "environment."

Tamara: That's too big a subject. Besides, we want to know what's going on here.

Others joined in with:

"Maybe we can call the mayor."

"How about the librarian?"

Tamara: Maybe Brad's right. Is "environment" in the telephone directory? in the yellow pages? Maybe we can call someone.

Bob: What would "environment" be doing in the yellow pages?

Terry: Well, let's see.

And so the search began. All kinds of information—local, state, and national—was eventually collected. Then community speakers including members of the Town Committee were invited to speak to the class about community progress in "cleaning up the environment." Activities rippled from this read-aloud for months.

Talking about books, book talks, is another way for children to confirm their learning. Reading logs and summary cards might be considered the written equivalent of such talks. Book talks can be done with the whole class or in small groups. If the talk group is less than class size, students may gather in a book talk circle. One student may begin by sharing an idea from the read-aloud book. To encourage volunteers, Ms. Elsey sometimes begins the book talk herself and then moves around the circle drawing readers into the discussion with a question or observation.

Book talks may, at times, focus directly on the development of skills such as those identified in Chapters 1 and 2.

READ-ALOUD 7: THE BARD OF AVON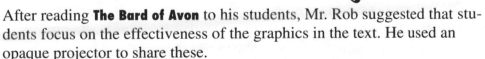

After reading **The Bard of Avon** to his students, Mr. Rob suggested that students focus on the effectiveness of the graphics in the text. He used an opaque projector to share these.

The question, "What do the illustrations in **The Bard of Avon** tell you about Shakespeare's time that you don't learn from the narrative?" had everyone peering closely at each page and comparing text to illustration.

Students' Responses

Susan started with the general observation that she didn't think she could fully appreciate the Globe Theatre without the illustrations in the text. Someone else followed with the comments that the illustrations made the dress and the buildings of Shakespeare's time clearer.

Bill, who was studying words and illustrations very carefully, observed that "To say that the cart of traveling actors rolled into the town square isn't enough to help me 'see' the scene. In the drawing I see the people as they dressed at that time and I see this small company of actors coming into town. Some are on horses and some are on foot. They carry their belongings and probably their play costumes and props in this funny cart that I would never imagine in a hundred years. It has a covering held up by—it looks like a joker's mask, of all things."

Fran: I think I need to have the words and to see the pictures too to really understand Shakespeare and his times.

Mark interrupted at this point, "Remember, Mr. Rob, when we were talking about my research project on hypnosis, I said that I learned more from the book without pictures than I learned from the encyclopedia, and **that** had pictures in it. I compared the information from the two books and that's how I found out that sometimes you can learn more from words than the pictures."

Often book talks lead students like Mark and their teachers to focus on research and study skills. Learning these in conjunction with content area materials give them purpose and meaning. Mark guided his teacher to help him develop his ability to compare and contrast the quality of information found in various sources.

The following conversation exemplifies how teaching research skills—here, comparing and contrasting—results because the need to use them grows naturally from the study of nonfiction material.

TEACHER-STUDENT BOOK TALK

Mr. Rob had dialogued with fourteen-year-old Mark, in order to alert him to the elements of an effective text from which to gather information for his research report. Each student in his class was required to complete four research projects during the school year. The purpose for these projects included gathering factual information but also learning how to write research reports. Four were required because each focused on a different research skill. The first research report concentrated on how to find and select appropriate information from reference materials. Students were fascinated when they learned the difference between paraphrasing and plagiarism. The second report of the year reviewed the use of these skills and concentrated on creating narrative text using their own language. In the second report creating a proper bibliography was also a goal. Students were encouraged to write longer and more detailed texts in their third and fourth research reports. Many of the children enjoyed this because as one fourteen-year-old said, "This is like writing a chapter book." Among the references that Mr. Rob used to help him decide which research or study skills were appropriate to teach his students was his own copy of Walter Pauk's **How to Study in College.** Mr. Rob guided students to get into their topics sometimes in small groups but more often individually. One conversation with Mark began with Mark's identifying his topic, "hypnosis." Mark found some problems that people had—phobias—and researched how hypnosis could help.

Mr. Rob: How did you get the information, Mark?

Mark: Well, um, well I got most of it out of **Applied Hypnosis** by Benjamin Wallace.

Mr. Rob: What kind of a book is that?

Mark: It's reference—literature.

Mr. Rob: Where did you get the rest of the information?

Mark: From the **Encyclopaedia Britannica.**

Mr. Rob: What made you select those two books?

Mark: Well, I had the **Encyclopaedia Britannica** at home, so I looked it up there. Then when I went to the library I looked up all kinds of hypnosis books.

Mr. Rob: Talk about how you feel about the information in the book **Applied Hypnosis?**

Mark: Well, it was much easier to understand than the encyclopedia.

Mr. Rob: Why?

Mark: Because it had everything sectioned off, and it had a whole little section about what I wanted to know.

Mr. Rob: So it was categorized.

Mark: According to the phobias and things.

Mr. Rob: And the encyclopedia?

Mark: Well, it really didn't tell that much about it. It had the history, so—

Mr. Rob: So, Wallace's book was far more useful.

Mark: Yes. Wallace's book. Well, I wanted to know more about hypnosis after I read it. I wanted to go deeper into the subject. I wanted to find out more about applied hypnosis. Wallace seems to know a lot about the subject.

Mr. Rob: I guess the writing style of Wallace's book made you curious.

Mark: Yah. It sort of explained things better.

Mr. Rob: So the style is explanatory. How current do you think the information in this book is?

Mark: Well, it was written in 1979. I think it was the second most current book in the library.

Mr. Rob: So you looked for the one that was written most recently and found that the school library did not have books on your topic that were very current. What do you think might have happened in those years to the field of hypnosis?

Mark: I think it probably gets, um, it gets more um, well, the information is probably different.

Mr. Rob: You mean it is more sophisticated!

Mark: Yah.

Mr. Rob: What could you do to find more current information about hypnosis for your research report?

Mark: Maybe, go to a hypnotist?

Mr. Rob: Hum, yah, do an interview.

Mark: Yah. Ask him questions about the profession.

Mr. Rob: What about other written materials? What kind of materials would you seek?

Mark: Uhm—explanatory text.

Mr. Rob: Yah. Newspapers, professional magazines, journals published by associations that hold meetings where hypnotists gather to discuss ideas.

Mark: Yah. I can get some of these.

Mr. Rob: I have another question, Mark. Are you interested in becoming a hypnotist?

Mark: Um, I don't know.

Mr. Rob: Were there any other characteristics of the book, beside the writing that helped you get your information?

Mark: Well, I've studied it before, so I kind of knew

Mr. Rob: So you used your prior knowledge to help you. So that you can clarify for yourself the differences between the **Encyclopaedia Britannica** and Wallace's **Applied Hypnosis,** would you write the similarities and differences between the two books?

Mark: Sure, but why do I have to write it?

Mr. Rob: So the information is concise and ready for you to use in your written report. I want my students to be able to identify sources that help them best to learn about their research topics. Comparing and contrasting information from different sources should help you do that.

Mark produced the sheet in Figure 4-3 to illustrate, in written form, what he had learned about the differences between texts.

APLIED Hypnosis
and Encyclopedia Britanica

Similaritis   Diferences
had sections-at   Britanica had
least paragrafs   history
said some of the   Apleid Hypnosis did
  same things   not have history

Aplied History had chapters and
more detail could understand

Encyclopedia Britanica
No chaptes chapters
No detalcs
hard to understand

4-3

READ-ALOUD 8: TIMMY O'DOWD AND THE BIG DITCH, A STORY OF THE GLORY DAYS ON THE OLD ERIE CANAL

Mr. Rob's class was studying the era of canal building. In his planning and assembling materials, Mr. Rob, was delighted to discover the fiction book **Timmy O'Dowd and the Big Ditch, a Story of the Glory Days on the Old Erie Canal,** which he read to the class. He had suggested that students gather facts from encyclopedias, almanacs, and history texts about this period of American history. The Timmy O'Dowd book seemed to make very personal and human the canal building and canal maintaining chores.

Students' Responses

Students observed many differences between the simple presentation of fact-after-fact about a specific historical period (encyclopedia) versus a story that took place within the same period **(Timmy O'Dowd).**

The students also argued about which source "taught" them more.

Jim: I learned more from the encyclopedia; that's where I got my facts.

Jane: But I got a better... I don't know. (She fumbled for words.) I like to read about people. It was hard to keep the canal operating. I learned that from the story about the O'Dowds.

Greg: You know, when I look at my report, I think I needed both sources. The encyclopedia gave me a lot of information but the story did too. I could sort of put myself back in the nineteenth century and fight with the O'Dowds to keep the canal open. Jane's right, I think. Timmy's story gave me a feeling about the times I didn't get from the encyclopedia but the encyclopedia helped me think about the size, the length of time it took, the many people who had to work at it...

And so the discussion continued.

In summary, this chapter identified reading aloud to students as the major strategy for instilling an understanding and appreciation for nonfiction. Several classroom instances of read-alouds and the responses they generated were described. Responses included discussion about texts, searches for additional information, information-sharing sessions, utilization of fiction as well as nonfiction, play planning and production, and creative and expository writing.

Many reading and study skills were developed as a result of the nonfiction read-alouds. The following list of skills emerges from read-aloud strategies:

- building independence in selecting and discussing nonfiction;

- reasoning through oral language;

- summarizing information;

- locating facts in several genres;

- realizing that fiction can be a source of additional information;

- self-assessing;

- learning how to relate old information to new data;

- using the library;

- synthesizing information;

- comparing information;

- using information to confirm written text;

- playing with words;

- creating new words; and

- building vocabulary for reading and writing.

The following skills emerge from book talk activities:

- expanding ideas beyond those in the text;

- working collaboratively;

- using resources beyond the text;

- using visuals, graphics, illustrations, etc.;

- assessing the quality of nonfiction material;

- determining the appropriateness of sources; and

- appreciating nonfiction.

We leave it up to you to identify additional skills within the context of our vignettes. We think you will be surprised at all the reading, writing, listening, and speaking skills that children acquire as they engage in nonfiction activities.

CHAPTER FIVE

HOW WILL I USE NONFICTION IN MY CLASSROOM?

We know that nonfiction provides, promotes, and provokes many opportunities for learning content. We know too that it is a wonderful way to develop reading, writing, listening, and speaking skills. As it answers some questions, nonfiction leads to others. It provides the impetus for functional use of research and study skills. It can also move students to produce "factual products" of their own making as was demonstrated many times in Chapter 4. All

the strategies, skills, and products noted in Chapter 4 stem from read-aloud sessions. In this chapter, we will identify (a) strategies, skills, and products based on a class or group reading of the same nonfiction title and (b) strategies, skills, and products based on school-wide and/or community-wide diversified projects. A list of specific skills developed through strategies mentioned is included at the end of Chapter 4 and this chapter as well.

CURRICULUM-RELATED TOPIC: Explorers

Ms. Smith's fourth-grade class was studying North American explorers. Of the many books available to children in the classroom library, several students became interested in the **Eyewitness** book **Explorer,** delighted with all the facts they were served. Others reached for some of the volumes in the **World Explorers** series. Still others exclaimed over **A Dog Came, Too,** the account of the faithful dog who, at the end of the eighteenth century, followed Alexander Mackenzie across Canada to the Pacific Ocean.

Ms. Smith gave students ample browsing time to choose the title they were most comfortable with and most interested in. She provided a brief summary of each book and displayed the summaries for students' use. She knew that each title was written with a different audience in mind and had deliberately selected the books for a variety of content, style, and reading level. Some students, she knew, would be overwhelmed by all the facts in the **Eyewitness** books and would seek other sources of information.

Soon five children gathered around the tale of the first dog to cross North America. Ms. Smith had ordered multiple copies of **A Dog Came, Too** as well as several copies of **Explorer** and other texts. She wanted children to engage in book talks after each group reading. In order to have group book talks, each student had to have a copy of the book. These talks confirmed what students had read and clarified important facts.

Students' Responses

The text **A Dog Came, Too** attracted the children because a dog was featured

so centrally. In fact, Stephanie said she thought it would be a good book because it looked like a story book, and that might make it interesting especially if the story was true. Brian liked the fact that the main character seemed to be not so much the explorer as the dog.

The group busied themselves checking to be sure that there was a "real" basis in fact for the book. They confirmed that, according to the author, the dog was very much a part of Alexander Mackenzie's journals of his expedition. After they read the book, they each recorded important facts in their nonfiction logs.

When Ms. Smith found that each had read **A Dog Came, Too** and had logged their facts, she thought they were ready for their book talk. The five students brought the books and their nonfiction logs to the small conference table where Ms. Smith was waiting for them. They were used to these discussions. Talk did not lag; all five became involved in the discussion quickly. As they did, ideas among them began to link. Nine-year-old Stephanie started with:

Stephanie: I think this book is great. It is about the explorers and the dog who followed them. He didn't go in the canoes because there wasn't any room.

Brian: This dog wasn't their pet. He was sort of a wild dog.

Stephanie: Right. He wasn't a pet. He was a work dog. No one ever fed him. He got his own food, probably in the woods.

Tory: The book didn't say that. It said, here it is (opens the book, and points as he reads). He never had his dinner served to him in a dog dish.

Stephanie: Right. So that means he had to get it himself. And he lived in the woods, so that's probably where he got it.

Seth: I wrote that the dog in the book was like an explorer because he did all of the things they did. And he was also their guard. He didn't let anyone hurt them.

Justin: You're right. That's really what the book was about. The dog was a guard dog. And he ran all the way to where the explorers went.

Tory: This book sounds like a story to me: it doesn't sound real.

Justin: It is. Remember Mackenzie wrote about the dog in his own journals? That's what the book jacket said.

Seth: Hey, remember when we were looking through the other books? That one about Alexander Mackenzie and the Explorers of Canada had a lot of illustrations. Maybe there's a sketch somewhere of "Our Dog."

After Seth left the group to hunt for other evidence that Our Dog really existed, the discussion returned to how helpful the dog had been to the explorers, how important he really was to them and how many specific ways he was of help. As the group summarized this information, they traced Mackenzie's route on the wall map to review what kind of a trek it really was for the explorers and the dog. They began to speculate about whether a dog could survive such a trek.

Brian: No wonder he overslept.

Justin: What kind of dog was that dog anyway? You know, what breed?

Stephanie: He doesn't seem to be anything special. He's just a mutt.

Brian: We have a mutt at home. His mother was a cocker spaniel; his father was a French poodle. If you put those two dogs together, it makes a cocke-poo. Get it? **Cocke** r spaniel and French **poo** dle!

Justin: Yah, I get it. You put the two words together and you get one. If you put two breeds together you get a new one.

Tory: Are there other stories about dogs who do things like people?

Ms. Smith took this as her cue to remind the group of how they might find the answer to that question.

A Dog Came, Too, selected by students from a group of theme-related texts, generated a good deal of discussion. Fact-based, it added to information about the Mackenzie expedition a perspective quite different from other texts yet it did not minimize the rugged journey or the incredible hardships and weariness experienced by the explorers.

Students developed many skills during the book talk that followed the group reading of this text. In addition to book selection and discussion skills, students became involved in verifying the authenticity of the main character, verifying facts shared within the group by checking quotations in the text, verifying author's facts via other sources, individually and collectively listing facts found, summarizing information, and searching for other relevant titles.

Later, there were individual reports from three students who found other "brave dog" tales and two students who became fascinated with explorers' journals and the kinds of records explorers kept.

"Just think," said Justin, grinning, "my journal might be famous some day." "Oh, sure," said Seth. Everyone including Justin laughed.

Ms. Smith laughed too and said it may not be famous but if you keep your journals and read them from time to time they remind you of important facts about a topic and about the way you used your time. "They'll bring back memories too of the things your friends said—the comments that were made as you discussed a topic. Later, they may even bring happy memories or sad feelings. In a way, they chart your life."

The group thought about that for a while and then Justin said, "You know we're keeping two kinds of journals—the one we write to you about the way we think and feel about things that happen in school and the other where we write the facts we find in our nonfiction books."

"You know, it was kind of a neat idea for this Ainslie Manson to find out about Our Dog in Alexander Mackenzie's journal and then to write about him," commented Stephanie.

Brian joined in with "Yes, it was really clever."

Tory thought of the Young Authors' Day the school held the previous year and said, "You know, I asked some of the authors who were with us at our Young Authors' Day last year how they got their ideas but nobody said anything about journals of famous people."

Ms. Smith commented that "We'll have to add that to the possible sources for authors' ideas."

"Right," said Brian, "Then when Justin becomes famous and we're famous authors, we can ask him for his journals."

Grins flashed around the table.

To summarize, Ms. Smith, a veteran of many book talks, prepared for the talk by ordering multiple copies of books at various levels which she thought would be of interest and by enforcing the brief set of rules the children and she had set up for such dialogues

- You must read the whole book.

- You must come to the book talk on time.

- You must bring with you a copy of the book and your nonfiction log. You may also bring any other information you have about the book's topic that you would like to share.

- You must not interrupt.

These rules were always visible on a wall chart. When appropriate, Ms. Smith referred children to them.

Interest in **A Dog Came, Too** and other explorer-related books arose from the school program. Interest in nonfiction can also proceed from the teacher's interests or from the interests of the students.

TEACHER-INTEREST TOPIC: BALLOONING

Ms. Sweeney loved ballooning. She shared with her class the fact that she was a hot air balloonist. Although ballooning was not a topic included in her district's curriculum, it was related to such topics as air, atmosphere, pollution, and several others. Ms. Sweeney knew that her own enthusiasm for bal-

looning might be contagious and that the related topics were important ones in the study of science.

Students' Responses

When she remarked to her class that she loved riding in a hot air balloon—that launching, floating and landing were very exciting and that, although she had been up many times, she never tired of it—all sorts of questions greeted her comments about her hobby. She suggested that some students might want to read about ballooning so she arranged an exhibit of Gary Paulson's **Full of Hot Air,** and placed next to it the **World Book's** "B" volume and the easy to read **Big Balloon Race,** about the Myers family members who were famous for their balloon feats.

As she collected the books, she heard Marty say, "My hobby is collecting baseball cards. I got five hundred." This was followed by a question from Rob, "You know what mine is? Metal soldiers. My father and grandfather gave me theirs and now I have a lot of my own."

Talk raced on. Ms. Sweeney, after speaking with the librarian, began to gather hobby books, grouping together those about the same hobby. Suddenly, she had many small groups gathering around specific areas in her classroom and a number of children insisting that their hobbies were not represented. The search continued and volumes for her "brown bag exchanges" began to pile up. Ms. Sweeney had found these exchanges very successful.

The classroom library table was the place where the brown bag book exchanges were made. There were two brown bags. One bag held the book **Full of Hot Air** and the "B" volume of the **Encyclopaedia Britannica;** the other bag held the "B" volume of the **World Book Encyclopedia,** and a copy of **The Big Balloon Race.** Two children at a time participated in brown bag book exchanges. The children selected these activities during free times as well as during the daily two-hour time block set aside for reading and writing activities.

Ms. Sweeney deliberately selected different genres. She wanted to provide children with experiences in contrasting fiction and nonfiction materials.

Ms. Sweeney used a Post-It note to mark the appropriate page in the encyclopedias. She always wrote a guide sheet to accompany the sets of bags.

The guide sheet on ballooning read as follows:

Books about hot air ballooning are in these bags. I love hot air ballooning. If you want to know about it, follow these directions.

Before Reading

- Find a partner who is interested in learning about hot air ballooning.

- You take one bag.

- Your partner takes the other bag.

- Open the bag, read what's inside.

- Read to find facts about hot air ballooning.

After Reading

- Immediately after you read, write down all the facts you can remember about hot air ballooning.

- Check the text. Were the facts you wrote down reported in the text?

Ms. Sweeney scheduled time for discussing the materials in the brown bags. This was also a time for Ms. Sweeney to learn from the discussion what children had retained from their reading.

Steven and Michael took a brown bag and so did Jack and Sarah. The pairs examined the contents of their brown bag. Ms. Sweeney listened to their conversation, taking notes as she observed them.

Steven: What's hot air ballooning?

Michael: It's like flying, but in a balloon.

Steven: That's sounds crazy. (Opens the bag with the **World Book** encyclopedia inside.) This is the first time I found an encyclopedia in my brown bag and here's a yellow piece of paper on page 39. Oh, I see, this is the section about ballooning.

Steven: So! Did you get the same book?

Michael: (Sharing his brown bag). No, this looks like a story with pictures. The pictures are real. They're actual pictures of balloons.

Steven: Well, mine is an encyclopedia. Gads! the words are soooo little. It's hard to see them.

Jack: This book is about a family who are balloonists. Does your whole family do it, Ms. Sweeney?

Ms. Sweeney: No, Jack, I'm the only balloonist.

At this point, Sarah, called everyone to attention.

Sarah: Listen to this, everyone. The book **(Full of Hot Air)** says, "There are two basic ways to go about flying in a balloon. You can go high with your eyes shut or you can go sort of low with your eyes open." I think this is silly. How can you fly a balloon with your eyes closed?

Steven: Let me see that! (Reads the same words out loud to himself.) This is crazy. Listen to this! "Actually there's a third way. You can go high or low and open your eyes and scream!" I think this author's nutty.

Michael: Sounds like a joke to me.

The students' discussion clearly indicated that they were noting differences in genre, and were recognizing and beginning to appreciate Gary Paulsen's tongue-in-cheek view of ballooning.

Ms. Sweeney had prepared skill sheets on ballooning which she'd placed in wall bins. Joanne, another ten-year-old in the class who was fascinated by interesting language, completed

Joanne's Sample

5-1

Although the sheet requests page numbers, Joanne promptly noted, "This book doesn't have any page numbers in it so I can't write them down." Joanne also decided that the language in the book was so different that it might be a book that could be used to help her cousin speak

INTERESTING WORDS/PHRASES FROM *Full of Hot Air*	
Special Words/ Phrase_ Joann Wang 7/27	Page in Book_
next of kin - I think it means a friend or somebody	no page number
get braced- I think it means buckle up, because it said sit down and get braced	
close your eyes and write home- I think it means you won't be home for a while.	

English. Joanne explained that her cousin was coming to live in the United States. She was born in Taiwan, and Chinese was her native language. The words and phrases in the book were so different that Joanne thought it would be helpful. Without teacher direction, she wrote a letter (see Figure 5-2) about the book. How wonderful that this youngster was able to see the value of language differences.

Joanne's Letter

Later, Ms. Sweeney used words Joanne and other children had written to create games that provided practice and reinforcement. Such games facilitated children's learning and were very much enjoyed. Children themselves often made up some of these games or added other words and phrases to games they already were playing.

At the end of the day, as she reviewed the spontaneous and eager formation of hobby groups, Ms. Sweeney noted that a number of books exhibited could be categorized as either information about the hobby or information about the hobbyist. She also noted that children seemed to be using some books more than others. She engaged them in a discussion on what books seemed to help them most and used some of the same questions Mr. Rob used with Mark in Chapter 4.

The three books about ballooning dealt with the topic in very different ways—one lightly and narratively with tongue in cheek (Paulsen);

another very factually, like the "ballooning" account in the **World Book**, and the third, in a more personal, family-story manner **(The Big Balloon Race)**. Such different viewpoints on the topic held children's interest and expanded their understanding.

STUDENT-INTEREST TOPIC: BASEBALL

As the hobby groups formed one afternoon, several students had gathered around copies of books in the **Baseball Legends Series;** one student selected **Sandy Koufax;** another, **Cy Young.**

> 7/27
>
> Dear Anny,
>   Today I read the funniest book! It is called <u>Full Of Hot Air</u> by Gary Paulsen. The publisher is Delacorte Press. Mabe when I get to California ~~it~~ we can go to the library and look for it. I think it will help you improve your english. It has a lot of funny words and phrases. See you tomorrow!
>
>   Love from,
>   Joann Wang
> P.S. When you get back to Canada you could recomend it to your friends!
>
> P.P.S Keep this paper!!

Jeff, an avid baseball fan, picked up **The Story of Baseball** and immediately became fascinated with the chapter on "Signs and Signals." These students and two other baseball lovers were ready for a book talk two days later.

5-2

Students' Responses

The Story of Baseball was so chockfull of facts that Jeff could not digest all of them but he figured he had plenty to share with his group; the others had found out about their particular baseball "legends" and were ready to discuss their lives.

Looking at his nonfiction log notes, Jeff started the the talk.

Jeff: Did you know that baseball games went back to 1846?

Bob: No kidding?
Then noting Jeff's book, he asked "Is Cy Young in that book?"

Elsa: Is Sandy Koufax?

Jeff: Let's see. They've got everybody in here (he boasted admiringly if not quite truthfully. He continued his search while his friends called their heroes' names.)

Ms. Sweeney: (smiling as she listened to baseball jargon and catching the phrase "struck out") Personally, I prefer the great Casey.

Jeff: Who's that?

Bob: I'll bet it's Casey Stengel.

Ms. Smith: Oh, no! (smiling) A much more famous Casey.

Everyone looked puzzled. It was Jeff who noticed the twinkle in Ms. Smith's eye and frowned in concentration.

Ms. Smith: I'll give you a hint. Does the "mighty Casey" ring a bell in anyone's mind?

Bob: Oh, right! (grinning) Casey at the Bat. No fair. He isn't real.

Ms. Smith: Did you learn anything about baseball from Casey?

Many of them nodded.

"Maybe you oughtn't to let any balls go by," said Bob.

"You shouldn't be too sure of yourself."

"Casey was too cocksure of himself."

"Cocksure? What's that mean?"

As they continued and then returned to their earlier questions, they remarked that Casey probably would not be in Jeff's book.

Ms. Sweeney was enjoying her students' search for heroes in the baseball "history" text and the excited faces of those who wanted to see what this general information book had to say about their particular sportsman. No one was going to leave this circle without an answer to his or her question and Jeff was "king of the information mountain" at the moment.

Thinking again about the phrase "struck out," Ms. Sweeney made a mental note to return to the group later and suggest that they might want to compile a "baseball dictionary" for those in the class who knew little about the game. Searching for baseball tems from A to Z would be the kind of challenge that fans like Jeff and Bob would like.

Book talks develop from class and group reading of the same nonfiction titles. Such talks range widely and call into action diverse comprehension, critical reading, research, and study skills. Community-wide or school-wide projects call forth similar skills and add the novelty of beyond-the-school involvement.

COMMUNITY AND SCHOOL-WIDE PROJECTS: Share-a-Book Day

We know of several schools that have an annual Community Leader Share-a-Book Day. On that day, people from all walks of life—newspaper reporters, sanitation workers, politicians, businessmen—are invited to share the book that had a big impact on their lives. We were asked to participate in such a day at the middle school in one of our suburban communities.

Each invited guest received a letter from a child host. The letter asked that we share the most important book in our lives with two different classes of students. We were informed that we would be spending about half an hour in each class. The twelve-year-old who wrote to us said that "The reason for asking you to come is because you are important. We want to know if a book helped you get that way." The invitation asked that our response include the name of the book we had chosen, the author and publisher, and a brief (no more than one-half page) description of the specific reasons for selecting this book as the most influential in our lives.

We were met by our student host at the building's front door the day of the event. We were escorted to the school library. Coffee and pastries were served, as hosts pinned a flower on each of the reading celebrities. A schedule of reading times was posted and also handed to each visitor.

Student hosts had prepared information for introductory purposes. They also wrote several lines about the guest's book.

Susan's choice was **Teacher,** an autobiography written by a great teacher, Sylvia Ashton-Warner. This book is about Sylvia, who used teaching strategies that enticed impoverished Maori children in New Zealand to read and write. When Susan read that book in 1967, her feelings about teaching changed.

"I love nonfiction because I can find some things in the texts that apply to my life. **Teacher** provided me with the confidence to continue to use children's books to teach reading. That's what Sylvia Ashton-Warner did.

"The story about Sylvia Ashton-Warner's classroom, and the shared feelings about change that she had made were compatible with my feelings. I remember how excited I was about finding something to read that was written by a teacher doing things with children that I agreed with.

"Nonfiction is for me. I am a person who needs to see products from my work. I saw outcomes from reading **Teacher.** I used ideas from this autobiography to make my classroom a better place for children to live and learn."

Susan read four pages from the book **Teacher** during her visit. After reading to the students, several volunteered to share a book that made a difference in their lives. Those who shared spoke about the nonfiction books they had read that made a difference to them. Susan's influence seemed to be the impetus that stimulate sharing. Susan helped students collect information which they then analyzed and assessed.

Students' Responses

Later, students discussed ways to thank the volunteers for sharing. Several students' letters of gratitude were received following the session. Each of them, interestingly, mentioned their own favorite books, several of which were biographies or autobiographies. Some students wrote of the books they planned to read later on. Two of the letters included a rationale for selecting the books mentioned.

One fourteen-year-old spoke about the desire to read **Sorrow's Kitchen: The Life and Folklore of Lora Neale Hurston** by Mary Lyons.

Habiba's Letter

Dear Dr. Glazer:

I'm a black girl who is interested in my heritage. Some books about blacks are O.K., but many of them, I don't think are written by women who know about black women. They don't sound authentic when you read them. I think that they can't be accurate. You need to have the experiences to be accurate. I'm not sure if Mary Lyons was black or lived in Harlem. But I know, because I read it, that she studies women writers, and that's O.K. with me. I like to read about the lives of real people. It gives me inspiration. I want to do something important when I grow up. I don't know what it is, but if I read about people who did important things. I might find what I want to do.

Thank you for coming to my class and sharing your book.

Your friend,

Habiba

Collecting facts about historical folks is a natural introduction to interest in the people in the community. Ray had always been interested in Abraham Lincoln and after reading several accounts of Lincoln's life, Ray jotted down facts he thought were interesting. His card appears below.

UNUSUAL FACTS ABOUT ABRAHAM LINCOLN

His parents couldn't read or write.

He was 6 feet, 4 inches tall.

He said "thar" for "there."

He was messy.

He got married to Mary.

The kids were wild because he never

yelled at them.

He was moody.

A lot of times, he stayed by himself.

Famous People in the Community

After the Share-a-Book Day, Ray and other students began to think about famous people in their own community and they wanted to find out more about them.

Students' Responses

Sam: I can't read about our mayor in a book.

Jean: (following up) No, but we can talk to her.

Mr. Bronstein, the teacher, thought this was an excellent opening for discussing the interview process and interviewing techniques for gathering information.

INTERVIEWING

Interviewing can be very demanding. The interviewer has to record as he poses questions, deciding as he continues both what questions to ask next and what responses he should record. An interview format helps make that process easier.

Mr. Bronstein decided that one way to teach the interview process would be to share portions of **Talking with Artists** (Cummings). In this collection of "Conversations" with a number of artists who illustrate children's books, the artist introduces himself or herself in a "My Story" section and then the interviewer (Cummings) asks each artist the same series of six questions, starting with "Where do you get your ideas?"

After sharing the sections about several artists, Mr. Bronstein asked students if they thought the interviewer was really getting a lot of information about the artists and their lives. Students responded with a hearty "yes."

Then he asked if the questions Ms. Cummings used would be helpful with a mayor. After reviewing Ms. Cummings six questions, the group pretty much agreed that some questions would be helpful in talking to the mayor and some would not.

Bob: Probably, if we asked the mayor to tell her own story, we'd get a lot of information and then we would know what questions we still should ask.

Ellen: We want to know what made the mayor become a mayor. That's like one of the questions Ms. Cummings used.

George: And I want to know what the mayor does at the office every day. Ms. Cummings asked a question like that of each artist.

Sandy: I would want to know if the mayor has a family and kids. I liked the question Ms. Cummings asked about whether the artists had pets.

Rick: But we sure don't need to ask the mayor how she draws pictures.

Mr. Bronstein: It's funny you should say that, Rick. I think one of the mayor's hobbies is painting. Maybe you need a question to find out what the mayor's hobbies are. What I seem to be hearing from everyone is that some of the questions used with artists will be helpful in interviewing our mayor but some would not be. Let's review the ones you said would be helpful.

Mr. Bronstein wrote these on the chalkboard and then asked whether students had any other questions. As students studied the list, they realized how little they knew about the major's job, so they added a question or two and then all emphatically agreed that they should let her tell her own story first.

From the discussion, Mr. Bronstein suggested that after encouraging the mayor to tell her own story, they might want to have a list of questions ready to ask in case the mayor did not answer these in "her story."

Students produced the following guide:

INTERVIEW GUIDE

NAME OF PERSON INTERVIEWED

POSITION OF PERSON INTERVIEWED

NAME OF INTERVIEWER

DATE OF INTERVIEW

I'D LIKE TO KNOW MUCH MORE ABOUT YOU,
WOULD YOU TELL ME ABOUT YOUR LIFE—WHERE YOU
WERE BORN, WHAT YOUR CHILDHOOD WAS LIKE
—ANYTHING YOU WOULD CARE TO SHARE.

(If not mentioned by the Mayor)

WHAT INFLUENCED YOU TO BECOME A MAYOR?

WHAT KINDS OF THINGS DO YOU DO
EACH DAY IN YOUR OFFICE?

DO YOU HAVE ANY CHILDREN?

DO YOU HAVE ANY PETS?

WHAT ARE YOUR HOBBIES?

IF ANY ONE OF US WANTED TO BE A MAYOR,
WHAT SHOULD WE DO?

OTHER

THANK YOU FOR YOUR TIME.

STUGENT INTEREST IN COMMUNITY: HOMELESSNESS

While Mr. Bronstein's class continued to investigate interview techniques, Eleanor, in Mr. Rob's room, was talking about a visit she had just made to her aunt in St. Louis, Missouri. Eleanor had seen a number of homeless people when her aunt and she went shopping.

The homeless people fascinated her. She was curious about how they got food, how they kept themselves clean, who they talked to, and where they slept. Eleanor shared her experiences and her questions about the homeless with her class.

"I never saw people sleep on boxes. And you know what? They had blankets over the boxes to make the wall. All of the people had baskets—the kind you use in the supermarkets—and they kept their stuff in them. I wonder how they got homeless? Do they ever get a place to sleep except in the boxes in the street?"

Questions like Eleanor's serve as theme starters. Children's interest spark the theme. The issue of homelessness in our country is disturbing. It is, moreover, a continuing problem in societies worldwide.

Eleanor's questions inspired one child to share his experience with homelessness.

"I was homeless when our house burnt down. My mom and my brother and me went to the park. When we were going home, we saw a big fire in the sky. There were lots of fire engines going the way we were. We never thought it would be our house that was on fire, but it was. There we were, standing down the street from our house and the house just burnt up— just like that! And we had no house anymore. So we were homeless."

The dialogue sparked questions to the once-homeless child, Timmy.

"Where did you sleep?"

"What did you do for clothes?"

"Did you have all of your money burned?"

"What happened to your TV?"

"What about your goldfish?"

Timmy said that he slept in the firehouse, got clothes from the Salvation Army, and people gave his family gifts of food, clothing, money, and even new pet goldfish.

Curiosity about homelessness continued. Group talk resulted in a list of questions about homelessness that the class decided they would like to ask homeless people.

INTERVIEW GUIDE - HOMELESS PEOPLE

How did you get to be homeless?

What is the worst thing about being homeless?

What is the best thing about being homeless?

What is the most important thing you want people to know about being homeless?

Mr. Rob created a poster with key dates 4488 B.C. to 1992, charting events in history that resulted in homelessness. At the bottom of the chart he included the note "This information was found in **Homelessness: Past and Present** by Carole Seymour-Jones. There are three copies in our library."

Several students were amazed that in 5000 B.C., homelessness existed; others were eager to talk to some people who were homeless.

During the read-aloud time, Mr. Rob read Cynthia Rylant's **Angel for Solomon Singer,** illustrated by Peter Catalanotto. This is the story of a homeless city man and his dreams. This beautiful piece of fiction realistically presents the emotional aspect of homelessness.

Subsequent class discussion led to classifying homeless people in two categories—(1) those whose homeless condition resulted from natural causes (earthquakes, fires, storms, etc.), and (2) those whose homelessness stemmed from other causes. Children decided to make a community survey and then list on their Interview Guide forms all of the causes of homelessness they had found.

Concise oral language, notetaking, interview techniques, searching for information, reading, and summarizing information were some of the skills used in the class research.

The sixth graders' interest in the homeless led far beyond the classroom to the identification of local community leaders who were involved with homeless conditions. The students raised a variety of questions with respect to the extent to which homelessness existed in their own community, how much exactly was being done to solve it, and what might still be done. To interview community leaders, they compiled an entirely different set of questions from those they asked of the homeless themselves. Sixth graders began to understand and appreciate the importance of the questions that the interviewer used. They also gained some insight into the many complex causes behind individuals' homelessness beyond natural disasters.

In summary, this chapter identified a variety of strategies, skills, and products that result from the utilization of nonfiction in the classroom. Strategies that facilitated group interaction and collaboration utilizing the curriculum and student interests including extensions into the community led to the development of the following skills:

- skimming and scanning;
- reading for information;
- questioning the authenticity of information;
- discussing nonfiction materials;
- distinguishing fact from fiction;
- verifying information;
- recording facts;
- rehearsing roles in life (acting like an author);
- following written directions;

- making meaning from text;
- comparing and contrasting;
- noting details; and
- letter writing.

Additional skills emerging from large-group reading of the same material include:

- planning with and leading peers in decision making;
- recognizing the need for nonprint sources of information;
- using appropriate questions in order to gather specific information; and
- sharing performances and products.

Involvement with nonfiction materials over time enables students to develop all the skills necessary for becoming productive, independent, and enthusiastic information seekers, collectors, and users. You will be surprised at the impact of nonfiction on the development of many skills and on all aspects of the curriculum.

Our story is told. The format we selected seemed the best way to share with you our ideas for using nonfiction in the classroom. We've included real experiences with real children using real books. We've incorporated the development of skills integrating their use in functional, purposeful ways. We recommend that you read and reread the vignettes that describe children and teachers working with nonfiction. Ask yourself again and again as you reread, "What skills are children using? How did they emerge within the activity?" We beg you to integrate skill development with nonfiction books in your classroom. Children will learn facts, concepts, and skills concomitantly as they read in order "to find out."

LITERATURE MENTIONED IN THE TEXT

Aliki. **A Medieval Feast.** HarperCollins, 1983.

Ashton-Warner, Sylvia. **Teacher.** Simon & Schuster, 1967.

Berger, Melvin. **Germs Make Me Sick!** Illus. by Marilyn Hafner. HarperCollins, 1985.

Berger, Melvin. **Simple Science Says Take One Balloon.** Illus. by G. Brian Karas. Scholastic, Inc., 1988.

Branley, Franklyn. **What Happened to the Dinosaurs?** Illus. by Marc Simont. HarperCollins, 1991.

Burnie, David. **Tree.** Photos by Peter Chadwick. Knopf, 1988.

Ceserani, Gian Paolo. **Marco Polo.** Illus. by Piero Ventura. G. P. Putnam's Sons, 1982.

Cherry, Lynne. **A River Ran Wild.** Harcourt Brace Jovanovich, 1992.

Coerr, Eleanor. **The Big Balloon Race.** Illus. by Carolyn Crott. HarperCollins, 1981.

Cole, Joanna. **A Bird's Body.** Illus. by Jerome Wexler. Morrow, 1982.

Cole, Joanna. **The Magic School Bus Books.** Illus. by Bruce Degen. Scholastic, Inc., 1986-

Cooper, Michael. **Klondike Fever: The Famous Gold Rush of 1898.** Clarion, 1989.

Cummings, Pat. **Talking with Artists.** Bradbury Press, 1992.

Doubilet, Anne. **Under the Sea from A to Z.** Photos by author. Crown, 1991.

Frank, Anne. **Diary of a Young Girl.** Cornerstone Press, 1989 (orig. 1947).

Freedman, Russell. **Lincoln: A Photobiography.** Houghton Mifflin, 1987.

George, Jean Craighead. **The 13 Moon Series.** Illustrated. HarperCollins, 1991-.

George, Jean Craighead. **My Side of the Mountain.** Illustrated. Dutton, 1988.

Gibbons, Gail. **Fill It Up!** Illus. by author. HarperCollins, 1986.

Gibbons, Gail. **The Pottery Place.** Harcourt Brace Jovanovich, 1987.

Gipson, Fred. **Old Yeller.** HarperCollins 1990. (orig. 1956).

Goodall, John. **The Story of a Castle.** Illus. by author. Macmillan, 1986.

Grabowski, John. **Sandy Koufax.** Chelsea House, 1992.

Gutfreund, Geraldine M. **Animals Have Cousins Too.** Watts, 1990.

Heller, Ruth. **Kites Sail High: A Book About Verbs.** Putnam, 1988.

Hesse, Karen. **Letters from Rifka.** Henry Holt & Co., 1992.

Hill, Ann, ed. **The Visual Dictionary of Art.** William Heinemann Ltd., 1974.

Hilts, Len. **Timmy O'Dowd and the Big Ditch: A Story of the Glory Days on the Old Erie Canal.** Harcourt Brace Jovanovich, 1988.

Isaacson, Philip M. **Round Buildings, Square Buildings & Buildings That Wiggle Like a Fish.** Knopf, 1988.

Janson, H. W. and Anthony F. **History of Art for Young People.** Fourth edition. Abrams, 1992.

Knowlton, Jack. **Books & Libraries.** Illus. by Harriett Barton. HarperCollins, 1988.

Knowlton, Jack. **Geography A to Z.** Illus. by Harriett Barton. HarperCollins, 1991.

Lauber, Patricia. **Dinosaurs Walked Here and Other Stories Fossils Tell.** Bradbury Press, 1987.

Lauber, Patricia. **How We Learned the Earth Is Round.** HarperCollins, 1990.

Lauber, Patricia. **Living with Dinosaurs.** Illus. by Doug Henderson. Bradbury Press, 1991.

Lavies, Bianca. **Tree Trunk Traffic.** Photos by author. Dutton, 1989.

Leslie, Clare Walker. **Nature All Year Long.** Greenwillow, 1991.

Lyons, Mary. **Letters from a Slave Girl: The Story of Harriet Jacobs.** Macmillan, 1992.

Lyons, Mary. **Sorrow's Kitchen: The Life and Folklore of Zora Neale Hurston.** Macmillan, 1993.

Macaulay, David. **Castle.** Illus. by author. Houghton Mifflin, 1982.

Macaulay, David. **Cathedral.** Illus. by author. Houghton Mifflin, 1981.

Macaulay, David. **Pyramid.** Illus. by author. Houghton Mifflin, 1982.

Macaulay, David. **The Way Things Work.** Illus. by author. Houghton Mifflin, 1988.

Macht, Norman L. **Cy Young.** Chelsea House, 1992.

Manson, Ainslie. **A Dog Came, Too.** Illus. by Ann Blades. Macmillan, 1993.

Martin, James. **Chameleons, Dragons of the Trees.** Photos by Art Wolfe. Crown, 1991.

Marshak, Samuel. **Hail to Mail.** Trans. by Richard Pevear. Illus. by Vladimir Radunsky. Henry Holt & Co., 1990.

Matthews, Rupert. **Explorer.** Illus. by Jim Stevenson. Knopf, 1991.

McFarlan, Donald, ed. **The Guinness Book of Records 1992.** Bantam, 1992.

Murphy, Jim. **The Last Dinosaur.** Illus. by Mark Weatherby. Scholastic Hardcover, 1988.

Murphy, Robert Cushman (foreword). **Larousse Encyclopedia of Animal Life.** McGraw-Hill, 1967.

Parker, Nancy Winslow. **The President's Cabinet and How It Grew.** Harper-Collins, 1992.

Parsons, Alexandra. **Amazing Birds.** Photos by Jerry Young McKay. Knopf, 1990.

Pauk, Walter. **How to Study in College.** Fourth edition. Houghton Mifflin, 1988.

Paulsen, Gary. **Full of Hot Air.** Photographs by Mary Ann Heltshe. Delacorte, 1979.

Provensen, Alice. **The Buck Stops Here.** Illus. by author. HarperCollins, 1990.

Provensen, Alice and Martin Provenson. **Leonardo Da Vinci.** Illus. by authors. Viking, 1984.

Rawlings, Marjorie. **The Yearling.** Illus. by N. C. Wyeth. Scribner's, 1985 (Orig. 1956).

Rawls, Wilson. **Where the Red Fern Grows.** Doubleday, 1986 (orig. 1961).

Reynolds, Jan. **Himalaya.** Photographs by author. Harcourt Brace Jovanovich, 1991.

Ritter, Lawrence. **The Story of Baseball.** Rev. ed. Morrow, 1990.

Rylant, Cynthia. **Angel for Solomon Singer.** Illus. by Peter Catalanotto. Orchard, 1992.

Sattler, Helen R. **Tyrannosaurus Rex and Its Kin.** Illus. by Joyce Powzyk. Lothrop, 1989.

Schlein, Miriam. **Discovering Dinosaur Babies.** Illus. by Margaret Colbert. Four Winds, 1991.

Seltzer, Isadore. **The House I Live In: At Home in America.** Illus. by author. Macmillan, 1992.

Seymour-Jones, Carole. **Homelessness: Past and Present.** Macmillan, 1993.

Siebert, Diane. **Mojave.** Illus. by Wendell Minor. Crowell, 1988.

Simon, Seymour. **Animal Fact/Animal Fable.** Illus. by Diane de Groat. Crown, 1979.

Simon, Seymour. **New Questions and Answers About Dinosaurs.** Illus. by Jennifer Dewey. Morrow, 1990.

Simon, Seymour. **The Rock-Hound's Book.** Illus. by Tony Chen. Viking, 1973.

Simon, Seymour. **Storms.** Morrow, 1992.

Stanley, Diane and Peter Vennema. **The Bard of Avon: The Story of Shakespeare.** Illus. by Diane Stanley. Morrow, 1992.

Symes, Dr. R. F. and Dr. R. R. Harding. **Crystal & Gem.** Illustrated. Knopf, 1991.

Thayer, Ernest. **Casey at the Bat: A Centennial Edition.** Illus. by Barry Moser. Godine, 1988. (orig. 1888).

Turner, Robyn Montana. **Rosa Bonheur.** Illustrated. Little Brown, 1991.

Wallace, Benjamin. **Applied Hypnosis: An Overview.** Nelson-Hall, 1979.

Waters, Kate. **Sarah Morton's Day.** Photos by Russ Kendall. Scholastic, Inc., 1989.

Wiewandt, Thomas. **The Hidden Life of the Desert.** Crown, 1990.

Wright, Sylvia. **The Age of Chivalry.** Kingfisher Books, Ltd. 1987.

PROFESSIONAL BIBLIOGRAPHY

Cullinan, Bernice E., ed. **Fact and Fiction: Literature Across the Curriculum.** Newark, DE.: International Reading Association, 1993.

Freeman, Evelyn B. and Diane Goetz Person. **Using Nonfiction Trade Books in the Elementary Classroom from Ants to Zeppelins.** Urbana: National Council of Teachers of English, 1992.

Hearne, Betsy. "Think of an Eel," **The Bulletin of the Center for Children's Books,** Vol. 46, No. 9 (May 1993), 273-274.

Kobrin, Beverly. **Eyeopeners!** New York: Penguin Books, 1988.

Lasky, Kathryn. "Shuttling Through Realities: The Warp and Weft of Fantasy and Nonfiction Writing," **The New Advocate,** Vol. 6, No. 4 (Fall 1993), 235-242.

May, Jill, ed. Special Section, "Non-fiction as literature," **The Children's Literature Association Quarterly** Vol. 12, No. 4 (Winter 1987), 165-190.

Short, Kathy G. & Junardi Armstrong. "Moving Toward Inquiry: Integrating Literature Into the Science Curriculum," **The New Advocate**, Vol. 6, No. 3 (Summer 1993), 183-199.

Strube, Penny. **Theme Studies: A Practical Guide.** New York: Scholastic Inc., 1993.

Zarnowsky, Myra. **Learning about Biographies.** Urbana: National Council of Teachers of English, 1990.